BORN IN 1953

HOW TIMES HAVE CHANGED

ELIZABETH ABSALOM & MALCOLM WATSON

D'AZUR PUBLISHING

BORN IN 1953
HOW TIMES HAVE CHANGED

Published by D'Azur Publishing 2022
D'Azur Publishing is a Division of D'Azur Limited

First published in Great Britain in 2022 by D'Azur Limited
Contact: info@d-azur.com Visit www.yearbooks.d-azur.com
2nd Edition Published August 2022
ISBN 9798843355944

ACKNOWLEDGEMENTS
The publisher wishes to acknowledge the following people and sources:

British Newspaper Archive; The Times Archive; Front Cover Malcolm Watson; p5 Patronicus; p5 The Gowertonian Society; p7 Spitalfields Life; p9 The History Press; p9 Darren Lumbroso; p11 York Castle Museum; p19 British Army Report; p21 CSS Group; p21 Pearl-Guide.com; p21 Western Australia Museum; p23 BAE Systems; p27 SS Maritime.com; P31 londoncouncils.gov.uk; P32 Richard Cannon; P33 www.planet-sputnik.com/ english-rose-kitchen-blog; FineArtAmerica; P38 blue17.co.uk; P39 Prisma Watches; P40 The estate of John Hopkins, Bill Brant; P41 Butlins; P44 Malcolm Watson; P48 Alexandre Prévot, DeFacto - Own work, p50 Victor Hugo King; p51 NASA; p56 eBat; 49 Quatro Valvole; p70 MacDonalds; p78 Vintage Dancer; p84 Science Museum; p84 JodyKingzett; 85 NASA; P85 Salvatore Barbera; p89 Eduard Marmet airliners.net; p91 Wadhurst History Society; p106 Atreyu own work; p106 David Merrett; p107 YouTube; p109 Cédric Janodet; p109 Ken Fielding; p115 Juan Solis; p121 Ethical Trekkin; p121 davidoffnorthide; p125 Corporate Finance Institute; p127 Kingkongphoto; p122 This file is licensed under the Creative Commons Attribution 2.5 Generic license; p135 The Step Blog; p139 Klaviyo; p139 Freshexchange.com; p140 Netflix; p141 Alex Needham ; p141 Willie Duggan; p143 Dan Heap ; p143 Sergeant Rupert Frere; p144 Dave Comeau; p145 John Douglas

Whilst we have made every effort to contact copyright holders, should we have made any omission, please contact us so that we can make the appropriate acknowledgement.

CONTENTS

LIFE IN

Monarch: Queen Elizabeth II   Prime Minister: Sir Winston Churchill – Conservative (Knighted on 24 April)

In 1953, Winston Churchill was presiding over a period of rapid growth and increasing prosperity after the sombre years of the war. Towns and cities were reshaped by a massive building programme of council estates, tower blocks and shopping centres.

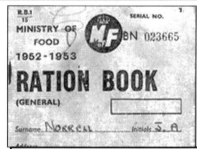

Rationing was still in place for some meats but most of the wartime restrictions had been lifted and life was becoming more comfortable. For the first time since the war petrol was off ration and a huge influx of cars took to the roads. Television sets mushroomed, taking up their now familiar place as the focal point of the 'sitting room' and the strange looking H-shaped aerials were clamped firmly to the chimney-stacks.

It was the year of the devastating North Sea Floods; the era of nuclear armament, Britain's atom bomb and the Cold War. Queen Elizabeth II was crowned; Mount Everest was conquered; the Korean War ended but British soldiers saw action in Egypt, Malaya and Kenya.

Hundreds died in the North Sea Floods

FAMOUS PEOPLE WHO WERE BORN IN 1953

20th April: Sebastian Foulkes, Novelist
6th May: Tony Blair, Politician
6th May: Graeme Souness, Scottish footballer
19th May: Victoria Wood, Performer
26th May: Michael Portillo, Politician
8th Aug: Nigel Mansell, Racing Driver
12th Oct: Les Dennis, Actor & Presenter
21st Oct: Peter Mandelson, Politician
16th Nov: Gryff Rhys Jones, Actor & writer

FAMOUS PEOPLE WHO DIED IN 1953

2nd Jan: Guccio Gucci, Founder of Fashion House
5th Mar: Joseph Stalin, Soviet leader
5th Mar: Sergei Prokofiev, Russian composer
24th March: Queen Mary, Consort of King George V
16th July: Hilaire Belloc, French born writer
28th Sep: Edwin Hubble, American astronomer
8th Oct: Kathleen Ferrier, British Contralto
9th Nov: Dylan Thomas, Welsh poet
27th Nov: Eugene O'Neill, Nobel Prize Laureate

1953

In 1953, the standard rate of income tax was 47.5%; sweet rationing ended; the first James Bond novel, 'Casino Royale' was published by Ian Fleming; women applied 'Pancake Make-up' with a damp sponge and scarlet lipstick was the norm; duvets hadn't been heard of and beds had sheets and layers of blankets, all topped off with a nice thick eiderdown. Bedroom were very cold ... on frosty nights, ice formed on the inside of the windows!; pubs closed at 10pm, and everybody seemed to smoke!

School boys wore short trousers and knee length socks, held up by elastic garters, and peaked school caps. Girls wore gym slips, shirts and ties and hats, and both wore blazers with the school badge.

Bombing during the war and the continuing demolition of urban slums meant more houses than ever were needed in a very short time. Council houses were the answer and in 1953 the country was undergoing a huge building programme set up by the government with a target of 300,000 new homes to be built each year. Central heating in houses was very rare and it was coal fires downstairs and electric fires or paraffin lamps, upstairs.

How Much Did It Cost?

The Average Pay:	£9 5s (£9.25) a week
The Average House:	£1,891
Loaf of White Bread:	7½d (3p)
Pint of Milk:	7d (3p)
Pint of Beer:	1s 11d (10p)
Dozen Eggs:	3s – 5s (15-25p)
Gallon of Petrol:	4s 6½d (23p)
Newspapers:	1½d–4d (up to 1½p)
To post a letter in UK:	2½d (1p)
B&W TV Licence:	£4 pa incl radio

Born in 1953, you were one of 50.75 million people living in Britain and your life expectancy *then* was 69.4 years. You were one of the 15.1 births per 1,000 population and you had a 2.8% chance of dying as an infant, most likely from an infectious disease such as polio, diphtheria, tetanus, whooping cough, measles, mumps or rubella. You were at the beginning of the country's recovery from the war, the decade that would transform Britain's social and cultural landscape. After the austerity, began an age of consumerism and when advertising was introduced on ITV, the nation could see the new products from the comfort of their own home. As prime minister Harold Macmillan famously said towards the end of the decade, "Most of our people have never had it so good."

JANUARY 1953

IN THE NEWS

WEEK 1   **"Demands for Tougher Action Against Mau Mau"** In Kenya, a loyal Kikuyu chief was murdered in the Government hospital where he was recovering from an earlier ambush.

"52 Killed in Belfast Air Crash" A BEA aircraft crashed at Nutt's Corner airport, Belfast, and 27 people were killed. There were eight survivors.

WEEK 2   **"George Cross for Sergeant Fairfax"** The hero of the roof-top gun battle in which PC Miles was killed by Christopher Craig, is the first Met Police Officer to be awarded the George Cross.

"Two Day Fog Over the Country" A thick fog belt, in places 70 miles deep, extended the length of England. Traffic was held up and Atlantic flights cancelled.

WEEK 3   **"British Arrest Nazis"** Seven ringleaders of a group of former leading Nazis infiltrating the German political parties, have been arrested by the British authorities in Germany.

"Controls on Cereals Removed" Subsidies and restrictions on type of flour will go, leaving a choice of whiter bread, not subject to price control, and the present national loaf, the price of which will remain unchanged.

WEEK 4   **"Derek Bentley Hanged for Murder"** Teenager Derek Bentley is executed at Wandsworth Prison in London for his part in the murder of PC Sidney Miles.

HERE IN BRITAIN

"The Rising Price of a Porter's Hat"

Billingsgate fish porters' retaining fee was raised from £2 5s (£2.25) to £2 15s (£2.75) a week.

Porters' special hats cost 30s (£1.50) in 1939 but now cost £6. 'Pushers-up' used by porters to help push their barrows uphill could be hired for 2d (1p), now 6d (3p) each. The man they took round to heave the packages on their heads charged 6d a round and now, 2s.(10p), 'Bobbin charges', 70% of a porter's total earnings, are paid by the customer for carrying the fish; 'shoring-in' money is paid by the merchant to his porters for carrying fish and 'foreign fish', 2d a stone, paid by the merchant on all foreign fish handled.

AROUND THE WORLD

"'Ike' In The White House"

In Washington, General 'Ike' Eisenhower was sworn in as the thirty-fourth President of the United States. He took the oath with his hand on two Bibles, one of which was used by George Washington when he became the first President in 1789. After the inaugural address the day was given over to carnival, with the President leading a huge procession from the Capitol to the White House.

In a break with tradition, he wore a homburg instead of a silk hat, *'in which sartorial originality all the assembled dignitaries followed suit'*, much to the regret of the Washington stores who had laid in a stock of silk hats.

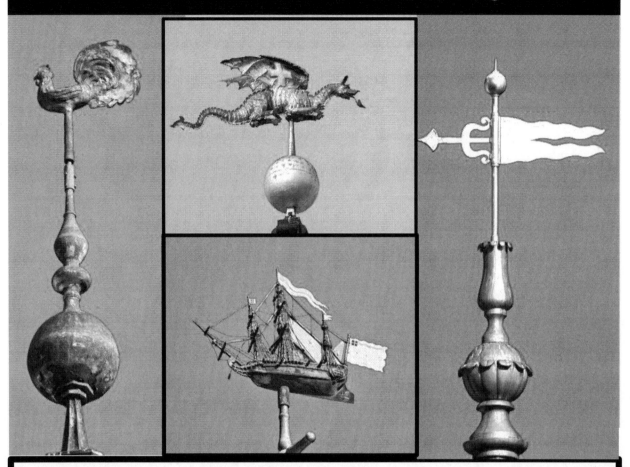

This month it was suggested that many of the weather vanes in London should be cleaned and oiled in time for the Coronation. The capital still has many weather vanes, but most are plain arrows on church steeples, usually with a rather wide vane (or banner) as the tail to catch the wind. Some churches vanes carry the emblem of the saint to whom they are dedicated, just as St. Peter-upon-Cornhill has keys as its design.

The tiny City church of St. Ethelburga in Bishopsgate has one of London's few remaining weathercocks, the cock itself forming the whole of one side of the vane, the other side being a banner with the date 1675. In Bishopsgate, above St. Helen's Place, the weather vane is in the form of a beaver and above the Worshipful Company of Leather sellers there is a fine antlered head. In Threadneedle Street, where the 'Old Lady' has no weather vane, is one of the City's most imposing, the giant grasshopper on the Royal Exchange. The weather vane of St. Michael, Queenhithe, a City church demolished in the last century, is now on a building near the site of the church and is in the form of a sailing ship. In former times its hull was reputed to hold a bushel of grain in token of the trade in corn carried on at Queenhithe.

Another ship in full sail can be seen on a building near London Bridge and close beside it, is a weather vane that takes the form of a multi-shafted arrow with a single head. From London Bridge you can see the huge fish that make the vanes for Billingsgate Market. Leadenhall Market has smaller twin cock pheasants. The Tower of London has many banners that turn 'with the wind, and the unattractive outposts of Cannon Street station on each of which is a plain arrow type of weather vane that has become a favourite roosting-place for starlings.

FEBRUARY 1953

IN THE NEWS

WEEK 1 **"Floods: Thousands Homeless"** Hundreds of people living on the east coast of Britain have died in one of the worst storms ever recorded and hundreds more are missing.

"130 Die in Ferry Disaster" The Stranraer to Larne, Northern Ireland, car ferry Princess Victoria has sunk in the Irish Sea in one of the worst gales in living memory, claiming the lives of more than 130 passengers and crew.

WEEK 2 **"Pit Pay Crisis Over"** The miner's pay dispute was settled with a 1s (5p) shift (6s (30p) a week) increase for 320,000 lower paid day-wage men.

"After the Floods, the Snow" Ice and snow affected roads in all districts of England and Wales north of a line from Wells in Somerset to the Wash. Only eight counties were unaffected.

WEEK 3 **"Mau Mau Strike in Nairobi"** An Englishwoman was among those attacked by the terrorists. Elsewhere police killed nine Kikuyu their biggest success yet against the Kikuyu gangs.

"Breakfast to Go Up" Controls are to come off eggs and sausages and rationing will end. The price of eggs is expected to rise from 5s (25p) to 8s (40p) a dozen and sausages to cost 4d or 5d (2p) a pound more.

WEEK 4 **"Deserters to Get Queen's Pardon"** An amnesty for 13,000 wartime deserters to mark the Coronation was announced by Mr Churchill.

HERE IN BRITAIN

"Sweet Rationing Ends"

Children all over Britain took their pocket money and headed straight for the nearest sweet shop as the first unrationed sweets went on sale this month. Toffee apples were the biggest sellers, with sticks of nougat and liquorice strips rushing from the jars.
One firm in Clapham Common gave 800 children 150lbs of lollipops during their midday break from school and a London factory opened its doors to hand out free sweets to all comers.

Adults joined in the sugar frenzy, with men in the City queuing up in their lunch breaks to buy boiled sweets and 2lb boxes of chocolates for their wives.

AROUND THE WORLD

"Ridding Australia of Rabbits"

For the third successive year there has been a favourable spread of the myxomatosis virus and the disease has combated the natural increase of rabbits.
In many parts of Victoria and in large areas of New South Wales, South Australia and southern Queensland, a 90% reduction of the rabbit population had been reported. In one district, thousands of square miles of light sand country that had been kept bare by rabbits was now covered with new growths of grass and herbage ideal for stock feeding.
Most of this county had been useless for sheep raising since the 1880s, when rabbits entered it from South Australia.

NORTH SEA FLOODS DROWN HUNDREDS

An intense depression caused gale force northerly winds to lash the east coast and break through flood defences from Yorkshire down to Kent. Combined with spring tides, the wind formed a fatal combination which claimed hundreds of lives and flooded thousands of homes on low-lying land here and in Belgium and The Netherlands too.

The first fatalities on land were reported after 20ft (6m) waves crashed through flood defences in Lincolnshire and then, throughout the night, the high winds travelled down the east coast ripping through sea walls and claiming dozens of lives. Water was gushing through streets; thousands of homes were flooded, and many people were forced to spend the night on their rooftops waiting to be rescued by over-stretched emergency services. Counties worst affected were Yorkshire, Lincolnshire, Norfolk, Suffolk, Essex and Kent. On Canvey Island, Essex, nearly 100 bodies were recovered despite the police compelling the evacuation of 13,000-residents in dinghies and fishing boats to safety.

In the aftermath, the Queen and the Duke of Edinburgh, visited flood-damaged areas in west Norfolk whilst thousands of civilians and service men worked to rescue trapped families, some marooned for more than 36 hours. They had to be brought to safety, fed, and accommodated. The bodies of the dead had to be recovered. Gaps torn in sea defences and in riverbanks had to be sealed and embankments strengthened.

Electricity and gas supplies had to be brought back to normal, and the water mains protected from pollution. Eastern Command arranged to deliver six million sandbags to Army depots; searchlight units were sent to enable work to continue during the night; bulldozers and Army kitchens went to the scene. Civil Defence food convoys originally intended to meet war-time emergencies were dispatched from Cambridge and lorries took thousands of blankets to coastal towns where the homeless had been accommodated in schools, hotels, and private houses.

MARCH 1953

IN THE NEWS

WEEK 1   **"The Big March Fog"** Thick fog covered large areas of Britain, disrupting travel and hampering shipping movements in the Channel. The Queen Mary, bound from New York was anchored in thick fog off Cowes.

"Stalin Dead" The Communist Party bulletin said, *"The heart of the wise leader and teacher has stopped beating. His name is boundlessly dear to our Party, to the Soviet people and to workers of the whole world."*

WEEK 2   **"Malenkov Named as Soviet Premier"** Like Stalin, he is a Soviet Imperialist, the Cold War will continue.

"Marshal Tito Makes Historic Visit" Marshal Josef Tito of Yugoslavia arrived in London, the first Communist head of state to visit the country.

WEEK 3   **"Farmers to Get £15m More"** Subsidies are to rise, ½d a gallon more for milk, 3s (15p) a live cwt (50kg) more for fat cattle, 1d a lb more for fat sheep and lambs and 8d (3p) a score (20) more for fat pigs.

WEEK 4   **"Queen Mary Dies"** The Queen's grandmother, aged 85, died peacefully in her sleep. 120,000 people filed past her coffin as she lay in state for two days at Westminster Hall.

"BBC to show 'Strangler of Notting Hill'" Scotland Yard agreed the picture of the main suspect in the Rillington Place murders, could be shown on television.

HERE IN BRITAIN
"Four Dead as Ship Hits Fort""

A Norwegian steamer ran into Great Nore Sands Fort, five miles off Sheerness, in thick fog. One of the seven towers collapsed and another rested on the deck of the ship, which went aground. The towers are not manned by soldiers in peacetime but by civilians acting as caretakers. Four of these men, who were believed to be on the sunken tower, were missing.

The towers consist of 36ft square steel boxes mounted on 50ft concrete stilts, standing about 20ft above high water mark and joined by a catwalk. Erected during the war, they are fortified with several guns.

AROUND THE WORLD
"French Alcoholics' Bill"

A French wife may be ordered to separate from her husband if he is found to be a 'socially dangerous' alcoholic. A tribunal will then fix the allowance she is to receive from his income and social benefits and will be able to send drunks to special 're-education' centres.

In the investigation of all crimes, misdemeanours and traffic accidents, the police are to arrange for an immediate medical examination to establish whether the act is attributable to the influence of drink. *"Consumption of alcohol is higher in France than in any other country, with grave effects in mortality and crime and in human misery."*

IDEAL HOMES FOR 1953

The Ministry of Housing has taken care to see that in this year's Ideal Home Exhibition, where many fantastical types of homes are shown, there are also credible *'houses and flats built down to a price and furnished, if not on the cheap, at least economically.'* The Ministry's theme is how to get a decent standard of dwelling at a reasonable price.

A cottage flat, planned for a middle-aged couple with a 15-year-old son has the expenditure on furniture for a living room and two bedrooms kept to £500. The effect is not of luxury but of something that, say, a Civil servant, on the middle rungs, could afford. Although the materials are inexpensive, there is plenty of colour and there are money saving examples by giving items dual purpose, a bedspread and quilt combined and a small vanity table that serves as a writing desk.

A two-bedroom 'People's House', intended for a family of four, including two-year-old twins, is meant for those who fall in the £450-£500 a year income group, and the actual cost of the furniture and furnishings on display is £485, or nearly £550 if bought on hire-purchase. The items come from the cheaper range and the rooms are not big enough to call for large items of furniture, but even with all the designer's skill, families in that income group might not find it easy to furnish the house completely in one go.

For the 'Elizabethan House of 1953', a settee and two easy chairs would cost £5 10s 6d and the total cost of 'modestly' furnishing this style of home is £1,100, *'not counting the television'*. The lasting impression for visitors might well be that their ideal home will have to await the ideal income! But they can see that what is fairly cheap need not lack taste.

APRIL 1953

IN THE NEWS

WEEK 1   **"Queen Mary Buried at Windsor"** About 4,000 people attended a memorial service in St. Paul's Cathedral which was followed by a simple, family, ceremony in St. George's Chapel.

"Christie Arrested for Murder of Wife" The nationwide hunt for Christie ended and he was charged with the murder of his wife Ethel at Rillington Place.

WEEK 2   **"Tube Trains Crash in Tunnel"** Nine people died and passengers were trapped in the wreckage on the Central Line when two crowded, homeward bound, commuter trains crashed.

"Britain Honours American Hero" Reis Leming, a 22-year-old US airman, has been presented with the first George Medal to be awarded to a foreigner in peacetime. He rescued 27 people in East Anglia during the winter floods.

WEEK 3   **"UN and Korea Begin Prisoner Exchange"** The Allies and Korea have exchanged sick and wounded prisoners of war. One hundred UN prisoners were freed under Operation 'Little Switch'.

WEEK 4   **"Sir Winston Churchill"** The Queen conferred a knighthood on the 78-year-old premier and invested him with the insignia of the Order of the Garter.

"Scientists Describe 'Secret of Life'" Two Cambridge University scientists, Watson & Crick publish their explanation of how living things reproduce themselves. They describe the structure of the chemical, deoxyribonucleic acid, or DNA.

HERE IN BRITAIN

"Queen Launches Royal Yacht"

Thousands of well-wishers greeted the Queen and the Duke of Edinburgh when they arrived at the yard of John Brown & Co., on the Clyde to launch the new royal yacht.

In heavy rain, more than 30,000 people came to hear Her Majesty say, *"I name this ship Britannia."*

The rest of her speech was drowned out by deafening cheers from the 30,000-strong crowd, mostly employees of the shipbuilders and their families. They sang Rule Britannia accompanied by a band. The Royal Yacht has a displacement of 4,000 tons and has been designed so she can be converted to a hospital ship if necessary.

AROUND THE WORLD

"Seven Years' Hard Labour for Kenyatta"

Jomo Kenyatta, the leader of the Kenya African Union, was found guilty on all charges and has been sentenced to seven years hard labour for his part in the organisation of the rebel Mau Mau movement.

The outlawed movement has terrorised and murdered countless Europeans and Africans for the past five years during its campaign for Kenyan independence, their aim being to rid Kenya of thousands of white and European settlers who have arrived since World War II and seized African land.

The Judge said, *"You have persuaded them in secret to murder, burn and commit atrocities which will take many years to forget."*

QUEEN MARY DIES

The Coronation of King George V

Queen Mary's coffin

The simple setting of Queen Mary's funeral contrasted with the sombre magnificence that surrounded the last journey of her son just over a year ago. No drums and marching troops escorted her to the grave but there were hundreds of cards, wreaths and posies laid out on the lawns or leaning against the chapel walls. Splendid and sometimes beautiful as were the elaborate offerings from Governments, statesmen, and corporations, it was the little bunches of garden flowers from private people who had loved or been grateful to Queen Mary that were most touching.

Queen Mary was born Victoria Mary Augusta Louise Olga Pauline Claudine Agnes Mary in Kensington Palace in 1867 to Duke Francis and Duchess Mary of Teck. Young Mary, known as May, was the great-granddaughter of George III and a second cousin to Queen Victoria. At the behest of Queen Victoria, Mary was engaged to Queen Victoria's grandson Prince Albert Victor but he died shortly afterwards. Queen Victoria suggested that Mary marry Albert's brother George and although it was an arranged marriage, George and Mary fell deeply in love. When Queen Victoria died, Mary's father-in-law became King Edward VII and when he died, George became King George V and Mary was his Queen for 25 years. Her eldest son Edward became Edward VIII after the death of his father and on Edward's shocking abdication to marry Wallis Simpson, her second son, Albert, became King George VI.

The Dowager Queen Mary spent the remaining years of her life devoting herself to many charities, but she also liked collecting jewels and she was known for wearing several dazzling pieces of jewellery all at one time. She would wear several necklaces, brooches, stomachers, bracelets, rings and of course a crown, often mixing diamonds, pearls, emeralds, sapphires and rubies.

MAY 1953

IN THE NEWS

WEEK 1 "Britons Home from Korea" Twenty-two sick and wounded British prisoners of war released from Korea arrived at Lyneham where relatives, friends, and tea, were waiting.

"Duke of Edinburgh Gets his Wings" The Duke of Edinburgh has been awarded his pilot's "wings" during a private ceremony at Buckingham Palace.

WEEK 2 "Lives Lost in Comet Crash" Forty-three people died when a BOAC airliner, flying from Singapore to London, was "knocked down by a tempest", minutes after taking off from Calcutta.

"Uncompromising Speech" Egyptian revolutionary leader, General Naguib, says the evacuation of the British forces from the canal zone should not be conditional or postponed.

WEEK 3 "Plans for Double Assault on Everest" Colonel John Hunt, the leader of the British Everest Expedition, has completed his detailed plans for a double assault on the peak, and has picked, but not named, his final team.

WEEK 4 "Crowds in the Mall" The Coronation route has been thronged for two days of sightseeing by crowds of up to 1m, who came see the city's decorations over Whitsun.

"Holiday Crowds in Storms" The south of England had one of the hottest and sunniest Whitsun Bank holidays for years, 89deg (32C) at London Airport. But Scotland, north and west England, the Midlands and Wales had violent thunderstorms.

HERE IN BRITAIN

"Mad Major's Swan Song"

In a single engine Auster, Christopher Draper, WWI flying ace, circled over Waterloo and then dived to make the final flight of his career … Up the Thames and under 15 bridges to Kew.

His reason he said, *"I am flat broke. I have been on the dole for 14 months and I was determined that when I made my swan song flight, I would show everybody that at 61 I'm still capable of doing a job. I think I proved it – don't you?"*

Unfortunately, he had to miss three bridges, Hungerford Bridge, Kew and a railway bridge because of bad crosswinds.

AROUND THE WORLD

"1,000 lb of Rice Reward"

Notices are being posted outside police stations in all the villages in South Korea, offering the reward for Lee Hyon Sang, 'Wanted Dead or Alive'. He is a philosopher, logician, university graduate and Korean guerrilla chief. The reward is equivalent to three year's free ration of Korea's staple food.

Seven other rewards of 200lb of rice each are offered for the 'philosopher' bandits – seven lieutenants controlling his Communist bands in other provinces. All bookshops are being watched especially for this learned gang, who make raids to steal arms but always prefer to *buy* their books for their hide-out studies.

EVEREST CONQUERED

Hillary and Tenzing after their successful ascent of Everest.

Although news of the conquest of Mount Everest did not reach the outside world until 2 June, the eve of the Queen's coronation, it was 29 May when the New Zealander Edmund Hillary and the Nepalese Sherpa Tenzing Norgay, became the first climbers to reach the summit of Mount Everest. They reached the top of the world, what Hillary called, *'the symmetrical, beautiful snow cone summit'* after a gruelling climb up the southern face.

They stayed for only 15 minutes because they were low on oxygen, but Hillary took photographs of the scenery and of Tenzing waving flags representing Britain, Nepal, the United Nations and India. Tenzing buried some sweets and biscuits in the snow as a Buddhist offering to the gods and the men looked for signs of George Mallory and Sandy Irvine who had disappeared in 1924 in a similar attempt to conquer Everest, but found nothing. Hillary and Tensing formed the second assault party in this season's attempt. They were using portable oxygen apparatus of the 'open circuit' type. The first assault, made on May 25 with 'closed circuit' apparatus by Bourdillon and Evans had failed. Col John Hunt, the expedition's leader, attributed their successful to advice from other mountaineers who had gone before, careful planning, excellent oxygen equipment and good weather.

Hillary was one of the members of the expedition led by Eric Shipton in 1951 that discovered the southern route to the top of the mountain. Charles Wylie, the Ghurkha officer who was organising secretary for the expedition and looked after the 350 porters and 35 Sherpas in the team, felt very strongly that they couldn't have climbed the mountain in the way they did without Sherpas and felt Hunt had been absolutely right to put Tenzing along with Hillary in the attempt at the summit.

JUNE 1953

IN THE NEWS

WEEK 1 "The Big Wait" Thousands of people spent the night on the Coronation route, having taken up their positions in readiness for the procession. They were not dismayed by showers of rain, and even sleet.

"Queen Elizabeth II is Crowned" More than 8,000 guests witnessed the Coronation ceremony at St Pauls. The Queen was told in the morning of the success of the British Everest Expedition.

WEEK 2 "Korean Prisoner of War Issue" An agreement was signed and concedes all the UN principles, except for the demarcation line on which the armistice will be based.

WEEK 3 "East Berlin Russian 'Emergency'" Demonstrating East Berlin workers clashed with Communist police and Russian troops and 16 died. The Russian authorities imposed a ban on all demonstrations.

"25,000 Communist Prisoners Released by South Korea" In defiance of the UN, and on the orders of South Korean President Rhee, the prisoners were released.

WEEK 4 "Christie to Hang for Wife's Murder" John Christie has been sentenced to hang for murdering his wife.

"Surplus Meat Off Ration" The Minister of Food, announced that an extra twopenny-worth of meat a ration book will be issued to butchers, who will be permitted to sell off any not required to meet the 2s 4d (12p) ration for registered customers.

HERE IN BRITAIN
"How They Celebrated at Home"

Portsmouth: Warships in port were dressed overall and illuminated. *Birmingham*: Many youngsters braved the weather in fancy dress parades. *Sheffield*: Coronation concert by the Sheffield Philharmonic Orchestra and Chorus. *Edinburgh*: A bonfire burst into flames on the rocky summit of Arthur's Seat and a fireworks display. **Hastings:** Fishermen staged a programme of old English sports, largely of a humorous character. *Chatham*: An ox was roasted. *Bath*: Processions, pageants and sports. *Northampton*: A procession of decorated boats on the Nene. *Nottingham*: A Coronation ballet with replica gold coach. *Beaumaris*: Fireworks and torchlight parade inside the castle walls. *Manchester*: A 21-gun salute was fired at Platt Fields.

AROUND THE WORLD
"… and Abroad"

Singapore: Clashing of cymbals and gongs, Dragon and lion dancers. *New Zealand:* A royal salute by an Army battery, the national anthem and a military procession two miles long. *Australia:* Thousands of new florins bearing the Queen's head were circulated. *India:* In Delhi, people partied on the hottest night of the year. *Pakistan:* In Ramadan, when Muslims avoid gaiety, special Coronation films were on show in Karachi. *France:* Tens of thousands were spellbound watching the ceremonies on television. *Korea:* The artillery fired red, white, and blue smoke shells towards the enemy positions. *Hong Kong:* Coloured portraits of the Queen, stilt walkers and colourful banners.

GOD SAVE THE QUEEN

Queen Elizabeth II has been crowned, taken the Coronation Oath and is now bound to serve her people and to maintain the laws of God. After she was handed the four symbols of authority - the orb, the sceptre, the rod of mercy and the royal ring of sapphire and rubies - the Archbishop of Canterbury placed St Edward's Crown on the Princess's head to complete the ceremony.

A shout of "God Save the Queen" was heard and gun salutes were fired as crowds cheered.

An estimated three million people lined the streets of London to catch a glimpse of the new monarch as she made her way to and from Buckingham Palace in the golden state coach and the ceremony was watched by millions more around the world on television. The crowds, many already damp from their night sleeping out on the pavements to ensure a prime position, were drenched in the afternoon by intermittent showers but despite the overcast weather, the RAF marked the occasion with a fly past down the Mall and demonstrations of affection by cheering crowds of thousands continued outside Buckingham Palace until late.

During a hush from the throng, the Queen delivered her speech in the evening and at the end, a great cheer went up, followed by the singing of the National Anthem. The Palace balcony was flood lit and the Queen came out with the Duke of Edinburgh to wave for another two minutes before she gave the signal for the illuminations in London to be turned on.

Later, thousands more young people massed in the West End to end the day, singing and dancing together. The showers continued after dark, but they did nothing to dampen the enthusiasm of this cosmopolitan crowd, determined to celebrate their new Queen

JULY 1953

IN THE NEWS

WEEK 1   **"State of Emergency Ended in Berlin"** The Russian authorities ended the curfew in East Berlin which has been in force since the riots in June.

"George Medal for Tensing" The Queen has approved the award to the Nepalese Sherpa in recognition of his achievement in the ascent of Mount Everest.

WEEK 2   **"Christie Hanged"** He was found guilty of killing at least eight people—including his wife, Ethel—by strangling them in his flat at 10 Rillington Place.

WEEK 3   **"Step Nearer to Korean Truce"** The Communists agreed yesterday to begin preparations for the signature of a Korean armistice. If the South Koreans resume hostilities after the armistice, they will receive no UN support in the event of Communist counteraction.

"Two Killed by Lightning" A man, walking across Kensington Gardens and a youth, on a boat on the Norfolk Broads, were killed by lightning during the violent storms which struck southern England. There was significant damage and flooding.

WEEK 4   **"Queen Takes the Salute Again"** This time at the Festival Hall Pier from some 150 craft as they passed up-stream during the Coronation year's, Royal River Pageant.

"Armistice in Korea at Last" It was signed in the great yellow 'Peace Pagoda' at Panmunjom, built of wood and straw mats and decorated with six-foot-high doves.

HERE IN BRITAIN

"The Big Bath Swindle"

Scotland Yard are investigating the plan to bring off the biggest betting coup ever known in Britain. A French horse running under the name of 'Francasal' won the 2pm race at Bath at 10-1. A few minutes before the "off" bookmakers all over England were flooded with heavy bets. When they tried to 'lay off' the bets on the course and shorten the price, it was found that the 'blower' telephone system exclusive to bookies was cut.

The Yard is satisfied that 'Francasal' was switched for another French bay, 'Santa Amaro' and the £350,000 pay-out facing the bookies was stopped

AROUND THE WORLD

"World's Most Expensive Grass"

New York's Central Park, home of the famous carousel, the boating lake, the zoo, the Tavern on the Green and skating rink, was 100 years old this month. The park, overlooked by some of New York's most fashionable hotels and homes, was created by a special Act in July 1853.

At that time the surveyor who inspected the site reported 'a marsh, inhospitably studded with squatters, herds of swine, and stump-tailed cows.'

There were no special celebrations of the day, the park was filled as usual with youngsters playing baseball, mothers with prams and young lovers escaping the August heatwave by rowing on the lake.

QUEEN'S BETTER BARGAINS

JUNGLE GREEN

Arthur Campbell

This month a lot was heard of 'the Queen's hard bargains' - national service men of bad character or poor physique whom the Services must accept as part of their annual quota. Much less is heard of 'Her Majesty's better bargains'.

The country has 313,000 national service men on full-time duty and 340,000 others in the reserve. This month a book called **Jungle Green** was published and gives an account of an infantry battalion in Malaya. The author, Major Arthur Campbell, recently commanded a company of The Suffolk Regiment during an outstandingly successful tour of duty and he describes the life which his men - most of them national service men - found themselves living, in the country where Communist guerrilla fighters have brought terror.

Since June 1948, some 20,000 British soldiers from sixteen regiments have been on front-line duty, searching out terrorists from the steaming Malayan jungle. Roughly half of these infantrymen have been national service men and of these, 67 have lost their lives and 115 have been wounded. For nearly all, the first entry into the deep forest is extremely frightening; insects crawling everywhere, ants and beetles of every size and shape and yet not one moving thing making the slightest sound. *"It was this eerie silence, which told on the men most."* The remarkable thing is that most master their fears and remember what their officers and NCOs have taught them in their few months of intensive training. Many young men are resilient, but it does not necessarily follow that these benefit as much from their periods in uniform as some older people take for granted. Is the national service man posted to Malaya luckier than his brother posted to Bicester?

AUGUST 1953

IN THE NEWS

WEEK 1   **"Holiday Resorts Full"** Blue skies and sunshine smiled on holiday makers leaving London and many other cities on the Bank Holiday weekend. Most resorts were full, and hundreds of visitors were camping out.

"MiGs Destroyer US Bomber" Russian fighters destroyed a B50 bomber and their ships picked up the survivors. A strong protest has been lodged by the American Ambassador in Moscow.

WEEK 2   **"Temperatures in the 90s"** The scorching heat set off many heath fires and thunderstorms in the south and west caused floods and damage.

"Greek Island Earthquakes" Helicopters surveying the destruction in Cephalonia found that all the towns in that island lay in ruins. It is feared that many hundreds of people have been killed.

WEEK 3   **"Iranian Coup d'Etat"** Dr. Moussadek, the Persian Prime Minister, was eventually overthrown in a US/UK driven coup by officers of the Shah's Imperial Guards.

WEEK 4   **"Buried Alive for 12 Days"** Two women were rescued alive beneath the ruins of their home, destroyed in an earthquake on Cephalonia.

"Shah of Iran Restored" The Shah and Queen Soraya who fled to Europe at the beginning of the Coup, make a triumphal return to Iran.

HERE IN BRITAIN

"Doing Porridge"

Prison Officers' are urging the abolition of 'No. 2 restricted diet' used as punishment, on the grounds that it is no longer a deterrent but makes prisoners fat and lazy. Formerly, it consisted of bread and water morning and night and a midday meal of bread, porridge, potatoes and tea. Now it is:
Breakfast: Porridge, bread, margarine and cocoa with milk.
Dinner: Bread, soup containing split peas, dried-beans, potatoes, carrots, salt and meat on any day in which meat is included in the normal diet.
Supper: Bread, margarine and cocoa. It was noted that since this new diet had been introduced, very little 'No. 2' had been awarded.

AROUND THE WORLD

"French National Strike"

France endured two weeks of strikes in their public services this month, the railways were brought to a standstill with no drivers. However, the warnings were ignored by tourists and thousands queued at the Channel Ports. Queues six deep and hundreds of yards long formed at Victoria station in London for the continental services.

British Railways ran extra steamers from France to England to bring back returning British tourists who were able to get to the French ports and travel agencies in Britain devised ways in which holidaymakers bound for Italian and Swiss resorts were taken by special trains which avoided the French railway system.

PEARL FISHING

A special Australian emissary has gone to Athens to look at the possibility of using sponge fishermen of the island of Kalymnos in the Aegean Sea as pearl divers in the Broome area, on Australia's north-west flank. The 15,000 inhabitants of Kalymnos, a small, barren rock island, made their livelihood in the past almost exclusively from sponge fishing, but during the last two years the trade has died, and the island is abandoned.

On the other hand, Australia, has the world's largest and finest pearl shell beds on its northern borders, and before the war had a pearling fleet of about 300 luggers manned mostly by Asians. Rather than readmit Japanese divers, they are looking for pearl divers among the Greeks.

Two factors will determine the practicability of the scheme, whether the Kalymnos fishermen are prepared to emigrate to Australia, and, whether they have or could acquire the aptitude for pearl diving. It is expected that a few will visit Australia so that they can see for themselves the kind of life they would be expected to lead and the greater rigour of pearl diving. The Japanese pearl divers are able to descend to as much as 20 fathoms below the sea level, more than the Malays who can descend to only 12 to 14 fathoms.

The Greeks will therefore have to face quite a strenuous test, but if the experience of the Dodecanese fishermen who emigrated to the southern coast of Florida can be taken as an indication, the men from Kalymnos should stand a fair chance. For Australia, pearl shell has become a good source of revenue and last year reached the unprecedented price of $A700 per ton. The occasional prize pearl, such as 'Star of the West', valued at $A14,000, is, of course, an additional incentive.

SEPTEMBER 1953

IN THE NEWS

WEEK 1   **"Electricians Strike Spreading"** More than 2,000 members of the ETU are idle. Strike action has been taken at two oil refineries, two atomic plants, motor and steel works, the radio and engineering exhibitions and the new White City television studios.

          "Dr Adenauer's Pre-Election Surprise" The West German chancellor has proposed a non-aggression pact with Russia to meet Soviet security demands half-way.

WEEK 2   **"Final Exchange in Korea"** The exchange of prisoners of war came to an end. The Communists sent back 12,751 UN prisoners, while the UN returned 74,000 Chinese and North Koreans.

          "Duke Does It" In Britain, Chief test pilot, Squadron Leader Neville Duke, established a new world air speed record in a Hawker Hunter with an average speed of 727.6mph.

WEEK 3   **"Disappearance of Mrs Maclean"** Melinda MacLean, the wife of spy Donald MacLean who disappeared in 1951, has herself gone missing from Geneva with her three children.

          "Francasal: Four Arrested" Four men have been charged in connection with the Bath Racecourse swindle in July. Two bookies and two racehorse owners.

WEEK 4   **"Ships Damaged in Gales"** Gales blew up over almost all the coastal districts of England, Wales, and Ireland. Ships were damaged, fishing interrupted and 'The Queen Elizabeth' was unable to dock at Southampton.

HERE IN BRITAIN

"Phone Calls Are Not Private"

The shared telephone service has problems. There are 600,000 subscribers, most of whom have separate accounts, but many do not. Subscriber A must work out with Subscriber B the number of local calls made, because any calls above the 'normal number' are charged to one of the sharers and he must then collect moneys due to him from the other subscriber.

Subscribers complain of overhearing, when the line is in use by the other subscriber, every word can be heard. One solicitor says he has to warn local clients that their matrimonial or business affairs are not a subject for discussion on a shared line.

AROUND THE WORLD

"Dior's Girls Hemmed In"

Christian Dior has been threatened with action because his seamstresses are working under unhygienic conditions with not enough air space. A spokesman said, *"Our 900 girls do work under impossible conditions, under stairs, on landings and down dark passages. BUT don't blame us! Blame the Ministry of Economic Affairs".*

The Ministry occupy an important part of the premises Dior bought in 1948 and were supposed to move out – but they haven't – and successful M Dior, has not room to expand. In spite of all his letters of protest, the Ministry *"Have nowhere to put their control inspectors."*

WORLD AIR SPEED WARS

Supermarine Swift WK198 breaks world speed record in Libya

Jacqueline Cochrane in her Sabre Jet

The official air speed record over a 100-kilometre (62.4 miles) closed circuit course was set by Jacqueline Cochrane of the US in May with a speed of 652.55mph in a Sabre Jet at Edwards Air Base, California. Next came an unconfirmed American record on 1st September by Brigadier-General Holtoner, of the USAF, with a speed of 690.12mph also in a Sabre Jet. *"Established in a heat wave and the best possible flying conditions".*

Then it was Squadron Leader Neville Duke's turn. He broke both these records near Dunsfold in Surrey, in a Hawker Hunter flying over the 62-mile course *"in the worst possible flying conditions-low cloud, high wind and driving rain."* This was followed quickly on 7th September, when in the same aircraft, Duke set up a new world speed record of 727.6 mph at Littlehampton in Sussex.

Duke had performed a victory roll over Vickers Armstrong Ltd., who announced their attempt by the Vickers Supermarine Swift F4 on this new world air speed record, would take place near Castel Idris, Libya, the following week. So only days after Neville Duke established a new world air speed record in Britain, Lieutenant Commander Lithgow broke it over the shimmering desert in Libya.

These sub-tropical conditions showed that great heat is a mixed blessing as whilst allowing higher speeds to be established, the high temperatures were responsible for many technical difficulties, both in the aircraft and on the ground. All the dry ice taken out from England was of little avail against the burning sun and the 180 degrees in the cockpit which *'nearly roasted'* the pilot. Problems with instruments and a 'bumpy' ride over the Garian hills slowed him down on some runs, but one of the Swift's earliest attempts at a speed of 737.3 miles an hour, was claimed as the new world speed record.

OCTOBER 1953

IN THE NEWS

WEEK 1 **"Mr Eden Returns"** He resumes his duties as Secretary of State for Foreign Affairs after six months' absence through illness. There is nothing to suggest any major reconstruction of the Government.

"Britain Sends Troops to Guiana" Naval and military forces have been sent to British Guiana; the constitution has been suspended to prevent Communist subversion and a state of emergency declared.

WEEK 2 **"Continuing Shortage of Dentists"** The Minister of Health warned of the most serious and persistent problems of the dental service and the hopeless insufficiency of dentists to cope with the needs of the population.

"New Atom Weapon" The 'Penney utility', Britain's second atomic test weapon has been successfully exploded at Woomera, Australia. Sir William Penney is in charge of the tests.

WEEK 3 **"Fuel Possibilities of Natural Gas"** Drilling in various parts of the country to ascertain whether there are resources of natural gas which might augment the nation's supplies is to be undertaken for the Gas Council.

WEEK 4 **"Strike Threatened to Halt London"** A creeping paralysis of the roads, affecting industry for 25 miles around London took place during a week-long strike by petrol drivers.

"Tourist Travel Allowance Increased" The foreign currency allowance for tourists is to be increased from £40 to £50. The unlimited allowance for travel in Scandinavian countries, withdrawn in 1952, will be restored.

HERE IN BRITAIN

"Hero of the Princess Victoria"

The George Cross was posthumously awarded to Radio Officer David Broadfoot, of the ferry 'Princess Victoria', which sank off the Irish coast in January with the loss of 133 lives.

The citation states that he *"deliberately sacrificed his own life in an attempt to save others. RO Broadfoot constantly sent out wireless messages giving the ship's position and asking for assistance. When the order to abandon ship was given, thinking only of saving the lives of passengers and crew, he remained in the WIT cabin, receiving and sending messages, although he must have known that if he did this, he had no chance of surviving".*

AROUND THE WORLD

"Miss Smythe's Victory"

Pat Smythe, of the British equestrian team visiting the US and Canada, won the first international jumping event at the Pennsylvania horse show in a field that contained some of the world's top male riders. Miss Smythe, the first woman from abroad to compete in this country was thrown by her mount 'Tosea' in the second round, but quickly recovered and rode the final round on 'Prince Hal' without a fault.

Great interest is being taken in the British team, as winners of the last Olympic championship, before they go to New York for the National Horse Show at Madison Square Garden.

BABY BOOMER CARS

Ford Popular

Morris Minor

Austin A30

Aston Martin DB2-4 Drophead Coupe

The Duke of Edinburgh emphasised the need for a vastly improved road system when he opened the Motor Show at Earls Court. This year, he said, it was expected that 400,000 new vehicles would be put on the congested roads. After congratulating the motor industry on earning £1m a day in foreign currency, the Duke also made some criticisms of modern car design. *"Why is it,"* he asked, *"that there always seems to be a handle or a knob just opposite the driver's right knee?"*

The great exhibition hall was packed an hour after the doors opened and the rivalry of the 'baby' cars tended to monopolise the attention of most motorists and would-be motorists – understandably, as the addition of purchase tax puts the price of even the most modest car out of the reach of many. These new small cars on the Ford, Standard and Austin stands were hidden by men and women trying all the seats and examining the engines and luggage boots.

Ford resumed their position as the supplier of the lowest priced car in Britain - if not in the world - with the introduction of the Popular two door saloon. The basic price is £275 to which must be added £115 14s 2d purchase tax. In comparison, the Austin A30 two door saloon has a basic price of £335, the four-door Standard Eight sells at £339 and the Morris Minor two door saloon at £373.

At the other end of the price scale the blue Bentley Continental was surrounded by admirers and the growing number of 100 mph British cars have been added to by the introduction of the Daimler Conquest roadster, the Alvis Grey Lady saloon and the new version of the Aston Martin DB2-4 model with the drophead coupe body.

NOVEMBER 1953

IN THE NEWS

WEEK 1 "All November's Rain in a Day" After one of the driest Octobers for years, heavy rain and gales marked the beginning of November.

"Guy Fawkes Day Rags" Guy Fawkes night in London was the most violent since pre-war days. Over a hundred people will appear before London magistrates.

WEEK 2 "Health Service Fog Masks" Doctors are to prescribe masks for those suffering from heart or lung disease and who live or work where smoke-polluted fog is likely to occur.

"Cleaner Food Bill" Powers to register all premises where food is sold or handled are proposed in the Food and Drugs Amendment Bill. The criteria for registration will depend on the construction, equipment and cleanliness of premises.

WEEK 3 "Twenty Die in Channel Collision" Twenty Italian sailors, including the Master, died following a collision between their steamer 'Vittoria Claudia' and a French motor vessel, 'Perou' in the English Channel.

"Queen and Duke Leave on Commonwealth Tour" The Royals flew from Heathrow to Bermuda to begin the first journey round the world by a reigning Sovereign.

WEEK 4 "Lords Vote for Commercial Television" Peers have backed the Conservative Government's proposals for the introduction of commercial television - despite fierce opposition from some rebels.

HERE IN BRITAIN

"Shilling-a-Tail"

More than 257,000 grey squirrels were killed in Great Britain during the past 12 months. Following the first anti-grey squirrel propaganda on Radio 4s 'The Archers', this is 90,000 more than the previous year and is in response to the campaign announced in March, introducing an experimental bonus system to complement the 7,000 squirrel shooting clubs - one shilling or two free cartridges paid per grey squirrel tail.

The Forestry Commission has disbursed about £6,500 in 'shilling-a-tail' rewards so far. Since their release in 1890 at Woburn and in the absence of competition and predators, the grey squirrel population has exploded.

AROUND THE WORLD

"Dutch Seal Last Flood Gap"

In the Netherlands, to the accompaniment of whistles, bells and loud cheers, the fourth and final caisson was successfully sunk in the Ouwerkerk gap, the last through which the tide had still flowed following the disastrous floods in February.

This last of the four Phoenix caisson had been pushed very slowly into place by nine tugboats and up to the last minute, nobody knew whether the extremely difficult operation would meet with success.

The tide, which runs normally at about 6ft a second, had quickened through the narrowing of the gap to nearly 9ft a second, and at times to over 12ft.

QUEEN IN A GOTHIC REVIVAL

This passenger lounge was converted to be the Queens private lounge

The SS Gothic flying the Royal Ensign on the prow.

The liner 'Gothic', in which the Queen and the Duke of Edinburgh are sailing on their tour of the Commonwealth, left London for Jamaica where the Royal couple joined her. The accommodation has been prepared for the tour and is now as it was when 'Gothic' sailed early last year for the royal tour which was cancelled because of the death of King George VI.

The personal state rooms for her Majesty and the Duke of Edinburgh are situated aft on the level of the boat deck. Immediately below, on the promenade deck level, the smoking room has been partitioned to provide the Queen's day cabin on the starboard side and the Duke of Edinburgh's day cabin on the port side. The Queen's day cabin has off-white walls, pale turquoise curtains and silver wall lights. The settee suites are covered with unglazed chintz. The Duke of Edinburgh's day cabin contains a mahogany writing desk used by Queen Victoria in the royal yacht 'Victoria and Albert'. Both day cabins are carpeted in dove grey, and each has an oxidised silver fireplace.

In the lobby forward of the central vestibule is an illuminated wall map on which the route of the tour is traced in coloured light and on which the ship's position on any day can be shown. The veranda cafe immediately aft the day cabins will be used as a veranda by the Queen and the Duke of Edinburgh and is furnished with oak tables and chairs upholstered in blue and dark red.

On the saloon deck the dining saloon has been divided and now consists of the royal dining cabin on the starboard side and the lounge has been similarly divided.

The 45ft royal barge is stowed in the after well-deck and is that used by King George VI during his tour of South Africa in 1947.

DECEMBER 1953

IN THE NEWS

WEEK 1 **"Nearly 2m Answered Strike Call"** All shipyards and more than 4,000 factories were at a standstill as men responded to their Union's call for a 24-hour strike in favour of a 15% wage increase.

"The Commonwealth Tour" The Queen and the Duke of Edinburgh aboard 'The Gothic' have left Jamaica, passed through the Panama Canal and are en route Fiji.

WEEK 2 **"Big Three Finish in Bermuda"** The five-day conference attended by President Eisenhower, Prime Minister Churchill and Premier Laniel of France, came to an end.

"Winston Churchill Wins Nobel Prize" King Gustav of Sweden presented the award for Literature to Lady Churchill on behalf of her husband who was unable to attend the ceremony, being still in Bermuda.

WEEK 3 **"Rail Strike Called Off"** The threatened Christmas stoppage was abandoned after railmen reached agreement for an initial 4s a week pay rise and promised further improvements.

"War Canoe Escort" The Queen and the Duke of Edinburgh arrived at the Fiji Islands in fair weather and exactly on time after their long voyage across the Pacific.

WEEK 4 **"Lucky 13 For France"** After twelve deadlocks, France has a President at last – at the 13th ballot in Versailles, Senator Rene Coty gained the necessary majority.

HERE IN BRITAIN

"Fresh From the Mint"

New money and Christmas are traditionally associated. The Bank of England always issues millions of extra notes to meet the demand and frequently the Royal Mint has to supply extra coin. This Christmas, so far as new coin is concerned, is one of the happiest on record. Never has there been such a variety.

Last year was a meagre year. The only new coins were halfpennies and farthings and yellow three-penny bits. But 1953 is very different. Every coin has been struck for circulation with the exception of the penny. The penny has been struck only for inclusion in the special sets of coins.

AROUND THE WORLD

"Trial by Wrestling Match"

Dr. Moussadek, on trial in Iran for his part in attempting to overthrow the Shah, told the court that when he was persuaded by his friends to leave his residence when the troops outside began to bombard it, he climbed a ladder and several walls before reaching a place of comparative safety.

"I am a man of weak constitution," he said, *"but believe you me, when I get mad, I am as tough as they make them. Right now, I challenge the prosecutor to wrestle with me and I can assure you I will knock him down in no time, and if he beats me, he can cut off my head."*

These remarks made even the Judges laugh.

Britain is entitled to regard herself as the world's foremost toy factory. We export more toys than any other country and at home, out of every shilling now being spent in British toy shops only one penny is going into foreign manufacturers' pockets.

Judging from the splendid array of British toys now to be seen in provincial shops and in the big London stores, the toy trade was never in finer fettle. Manufacturers have been able to obtain the raw materials they want, and the result is a profusion of new and original toys, and improved versions of the old favourites, which ought to satisfy the most fastidious boy or girl. Since the war there have been complaints that the prices of toys had become too high. This Christmas the public will reap the benefit of the reduction in purchase tax from 33% to 25%. This means that a toy which last Christmas cost 10s 6d (53p) now costs 10s (50p) and there is a general tendency for prices to fall, thanks to the availability of materials.

Compared with last Christmas, toys are either cheaper or better, or both. The best of them provide some answer to occasional criticisms of shoddy construction, and toys which have come here from abroad appear inferior by comparison. The emphasis placed this year on inter-planetary travel is too plain to be missed. It seems that almost any toy can be adapted to the space-travel theme, and even the malleable face of a puppet is recognizable as that of Mr Dan Dare, that most renowned of space travellers. Sets of "space men" in 7s 6d (38p) boxes are selling well, but this does not mean that any serious threat has arisen to the existence of toy soldiers who, of course, never die.

THE MAJOR NEWS STORIES

1950:

Feb: Clement Attlee wins the General Election for Labour giving them a 2nd term in government after their triumph in 1945.

Aug: 4,000 British troops are sent to Korea.

1951:

May: 3 George VI opens the Festival of Britain in London, including the Royal Festival Hall, Dome of Discovery and Skylon.

Oct: The Conservative Party led by Winston Churchill wins the General Election. It is six years since he was previously Prime Minister.

1952:

Feb: King George VI dies at Sandringham House, aged 56. He is succeeded by his daughter, Princess Elizabeth.

Dec: 4–9 The Great Smog blankets London, causing transport chaos and, it is believed, around 4,000 deaths.

1953:

Jan: Dwight D Eisenhower is sworn in as the 34th President of the United States.

Jan: Devastating North Sea Floods.

Jun: The coronation of Queen Elizabeth II takes place at Westminster Abbey. A public holiday is declared.

1954:

May: Roger Bannister becomes the first person to break the four-minute-mile at Oxford

Jul: Nearly a decade after the end of WW2, food rationing in the UK ends, with the lifting of restrictions on sale and purchase of meat.

1952: In February, compulsory Identity Cards are abolished. Brought in under the National Registration Act of 1939, every person, including children, had to carry it at all times, to show who they were and where they lived.

1953: On 29th May: Emund Hillary and Tenzing Norgay become the first men to reach the summit of Mount Everest. The British Expedition was led by Col. John Hunt and the news reached England on Coronation Day.

1955:

Apr: Winston Churchill resigns as Prime Minister due to ill-health and the Foreign Secretary, Anthony Eden, succeeds him.

Sep: ITV broadcasts the UK's first commercial television ending the BBC's 18-year monopoly. The first advertisement shown is for Gibbs SR toothpaste.

1956:

Feb: British spies, Guy Burgess and Donald Maclean show up in the Soviet Union after being missing for 5 years.

Apr: British MI6 diver Lionel Crabb, dives into Portsmouth Harbour to investigate a visiting Soviet cruiser and vanishes.

Jul: Gamal Abdel Nasser, the Egyptian leader, announces the nationalisation of the Suez Canal, beginning the Suez Crisis.

1957:

Jan: Anthony Eden resigns as Prime Minister due to ill health and Harold Macmillan succeeds him.

Mar: Egypt re-opens the Suez Canal and petrol rationing ends in May.

Jun: ERNIE selects the first Premium Bond winners.

1958:

Feb: The Manchester United FC team plane crashes at Munich Airport. 7 of the players are killed and an 8th dies later in hospital.

Jun: The Queen officially reopens Gatwick Airport which has been expanded at a cost of more than £7,000,000.

1959:

Jun: Christopher Cockerell's 'Hovercraft' is officially launched

Jul: UK Postcodes are introduced for the first time, in Norwich.

1956 Oct: The Queen switched on the world's first nuclear powered electricity generating station at Calder Hall, Cumberland. It was a fantastic engineering achievement, built within three years of cutting the first sod on the south side of the river Calder.

1958: In June, the first parking meter in Britain was installed in Grosvenor Square, near the US Embassy in Westminster. Parking for one hour cost six shillings (30p) and those who overstayed or neglected to pay at all received a £2 penalty.

THE HOME

During the early 50's, very few people had a television and the wireless reigned supreme. Daytime programmes were for wives, mothers and their children. 'Workers Playtime' continued to "come to you from a factory somewhere in England" and singers were interspersed with the major comedians of the day, Arthur Askey, Tommy Trinder, Charlie Chester and Ted Ray.

Music was important, with 'Music while you work' and 'Housewives Choice'. Soap operas gripped us, 'Mrs Dale's Diary' and 'The Archers'. Sunday lunchtimes meant 'Two-Way Family Favourites', music and messages for the troops in Germany. In the evening we could "Stop the roar of London's mighty traffic" and listen to 'In Town Tonight', and the children weren't forgotten, they had 'Listen with Mother', Children's Hour 'Children's Favourites' with Uncle Mac.

In 1958, Rowntree brought out their television advertisement, "Don't Forget the Fruit Gums Mum"

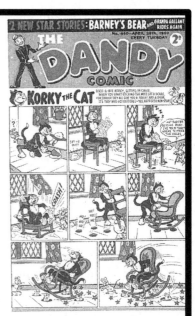

Sweets were rationed until 1953 but children with a few pennies pocket money could choose sweeties from the rows of jars on the shelves. Four blackjacks or fruit salads for a penny, a Barratt's Sherbet Fountain with a stick of liquorice in it, raspberry drops, dolly mixture or toffees. You could 'smoke' a sweet cigarette whilst reading Dan Dare's adventures in Eagle or laugh with Radio Fun, Beano and Dandy comics.

IN THE 1950s

The drabness of the war years gave way by the mid '50s to an age of colour and plastic in the home. Textile restrictions had been lifted and consumers were eager for new brightly patterned curtains and upholstery, but it was the kitchen that was changed most, with the introductionsof coloured plastic goods.

The concept of 'built in' wall units and cupboards, rather than free standing wooden units appeared but it was only when stores such as MFI appeared that fitted kitchens become affordable for most.

In 1952 the nuclear family was the norm, father out at work and mother busy with the housework. Less than 10% of households had a refrigerator, meat was stored in a wire mesh 'safe' in the larder, vegetables wilted on a rack and shopping was done daily. It was the time of spam fritters, salmon sandwiches, tinned fruit with evaporated milk and ham salad for high tea on Sundays. Salad in the summer consisted of round lettuce, cucumber and tomatoes, and the only dressing available was Heinz Salad Cream, olive oil only came in tiny bottles from the chemist for your ears!

Many housewifes wanted a Kenwood Chef to make baking and food preparation easier. And these new domestic inventions coincided with an upsurge in 'do-it-yourself' or DIY from the mid-1950s. The nation that had adopted a 'make do and mend' attitude during wartime privations took very readily to the idea of improving their homes themselves.

1950 'Painting by numbers' kits are first marketed by the Palmer Show Card Paint Company in Detroit.
The Festival Ballet, founded by Alicia Markova and Anton Dolin makes its debut performance.

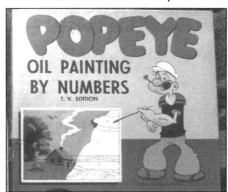

1951 Dennis the Menace makes his first appearance in The Beano comic.
The first ever Miss World beauty pageant is held as part of the Festival of Britain.

1952 The first TV detector van begins clamping down on the estimated 150,000 British households that watch television without a licence.

Vladimir Tretchikoff paints his best-selling work, 'Chinese Girl' sometimes known as 'The Green Lady'
'The Mousetrap' by Agatha Christie opens at the New Ambassadors Theatre.

1953 The current affairs series Panorama is first shown on BBC.
The 'Piltdown Man' is exposed as a hoax.
'The Moka', the first Italian espresso coffee bar is the first to open in London and Laura Ashley sells her first printed fabrics

1954 Two months after the author's death, Richard Burton makes famous his 'First Voice' in Dylan Thomas's radio play, 'Under Milk Wood'.

'The Fellowship of the Ring', the first of three volumes of J.R.R. Tolkien's epic fantasy novel, 'The Lord of the Rings' is published.

1955 Pietro Annigoni's iconic portrait of the Queen is unveiled.
The 'Guinness Book of Records' is first published.

1956 Harold Macmillan, Chancellor of the Exchequer, announces the launch of Premium Bonds with a top prize of £1,000.
The Queen awards Ninette de Valois's ballet school and companies the title "Royal" and they become the Royal Ballet of England.

1957 The cartoon character, Andy Capp first appears in northern editions of the 'Daily Mirror'.
The Queen broadcasts her first Royal Christmas Message on television.

1958 The first Duke of Edinburgh Award is presented at Buckingham Palace.
The practice of presenting debutantes to the royal court is abolished.
Both 'Grandstand' and 'Blue Peter' make their debut on BBC television.

1959 The ballerina, Margot Fonteyn is released from prison in Panama, having been suspected of being involved in a coup against the government.
BBC airs 'Juke Box Jury' chaired by David Jacobs, for the first time.

IN THE 1950s

SHE SAT DOWN ON A LITTLE BOULDER AND THEN BERTIE GOT 'A LITTLE BOLDER' TOO

1954, Donald McGill, the English graphic artist who painted and popularised 'saucy seaside postcards' was found guilty in Lincoln, of breaching the Obscene Publications Act of 1857. He was fined £50 with £25 costs.

The scenes he painted were most often at the seaside and featured an array of buxom young women, fat old ladies, drunken men, honeymoon couples and vicars, all displaying a fine level of social commentary and a 'naughty' sense of humour.

"I'm in a ticklish position here!"

FESTIVAL OF BRITAIN
1951

In 1951, the government took inspiration from the Great Exhibition of 1851, to organise the 'Festival of Britain' with the aim of promoting a feeling of recovery in the still war damaged country. Sited on the South Bank in London, the exhibits were to celebrate British industry, arts and science and led by a young architect, Hugh Casson, the buildings themselves turned out to be just as important and inspiring.

• The largest dome in the world at the time, standing 93ft tall with a diameter of 365ft which held exhibitions on the theme of discovery, the New World, the Polar regions, the Sea, the Sky and Outer Space.

• Adjacent to the Dome was the Skylon, a stunning, futuristic-looking structure, it was a vertical cigar shaped tower supported by cables that gave it the impression of floating above the ground.

• The Telekinema was a 400-seat, state-of-the-art, cinema which had the necessary technology to screen both films and large screen television and proved to be one of the most popular attractions.

Also built were the Royal Festival Hall and a new wing of the Science Museum whilst upriver from the main site was Battersea Park, home to the Festival fun-fair, pleasure gardens, rides and open-air amusements.

FILMS

1950 The black and white film, **All the King's Men** picked up the Oscar for Best Picture of the year. Based on the Pulitzer Prize winning book by Robert Penn Warren, it relates the rise and fall of an ambitious and ruthless politician, Willie Stark, during the depression in the American South.

1951 **All About Eve** starred Bette Davis and Anne Baxter and received a record 14 Academy Award nominations – four of them for the female acting - and won six, including Best Picture. It also featured Marilyn Monroe in one of her earliest roles

1952 Gene Kelly and Leslie Caron in her acting debut, had a huge success with **An American in Paris**. The climax of the film is a 17-minute ballet danced by the pair causing controversy over part of Caron's dance sequence with a chair. The censor called it 'sexually provocative' to which, surprised, Caron answered, *"What can you do with a chair?"*

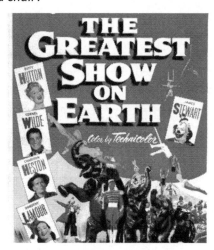

1953 **The Greatest Show on Earth** set in the Ringling Bros. and Barnum and Bailey Circus was certainly a great show. The circus troupe, 1,400 people appear, plus hundreds of animals and 60 railroad cars of equipment and tents. The actors learned their respective circus roles and participated in the acts.

1954 This year, the trials and tribulations of three US Army soldiers and their women in Hawaii during the lead up to the attack on Pearl Harbour won **From Here to Eternity** the accolades.

1955 **The Seven Year Itch** premièred and contains the famous image of Marilyn Monroe standing on a subway grate as her white dress is blown upwards by a passing train. **On the Waterfront** won the Oscar.

1956 The first and only entirely British film to have won the Oscar for Best Picture by this time was **Hamlet** starring Laurence Oliver in 1948 and the prize was not picked up again until **Tom Jones** in 1963.
An American romantic drama **Marty** was this year's winner and enjoyed international success, winning the Palme d'Or also.

1957 **Around the World in 80 days** was the first film to win Best Picture when all its fellow nominees were also filmed in colour.

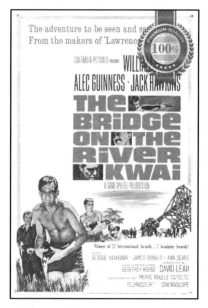

1958 British director, David Lean's epic war film **The Bridge on the River Kwai** won the Academy Award for Best Picture. British actor Alec Guinness starred, and it became the highest earning film of the year.

1959 Leslie Caron was **Gigi** and the film won all nine of its Oscar nominations. The screenplay, songs and lyrics were written by Alan Jay Lerner and music by Frederick Loewe was arranged by André Previn.

In The 1950s

British Film in the 1950s

If the 1940s was seen by many as 'the golden age' of British cinema, it was followed in the 50's by 'the dark age'. The two major cinema chains, Rank and Associated British Pictures embarked on a programme of cinema closures and admissions dropped by 500m over the ten years.

Even though no Oscars were won, there were good films: The most popular genre was the British war film. **The Cruel Sea, The Dam Busters, Reach for the Sky** and **Sink the Bismarck!** were top box-office attractions, while **The Bridge on the River Kwai** was the British cinema's biggest international success of the decade.

Some criticised the nostalgia but there were some changes to the traditional formula of male, stiff upper lip heroics, **A Town Like Alice** was shown from the female point of view and **Ice Cold in Alex** has an assertive female lead, the nurse who sorely tempts the neurotic British officer 'hero'..

Comedy was always popular. Ealing Studios produced **The Lavender Hill Mob**, **The Man in the White Suit** and **The Ladykillers** all featuring Britain's finest actor-star of the time, Alec Guinness. When Ealing closed in 1958, their gentle comedy was replaced by the raunchy high spirits of the **Carry On** films, peaking with **Carry On Nurse**.

The **St Trinian's** films had their following, as did the **Doctor** series, launched with spectacular success by **Doctor in the House**. **I'm All Right Jack** was a satire on industrial relations and **The Curse of Frankenstein** was famously described by the critic for the Observer newspaper as being amongst the most repulsive films she had ever seen. Quite a contrast to **Genevieve** and the London to Brighton car race.

At the end of the 50s, **Room at the Top** was a huge international success, and its sexual frankness and Northern realism ushered in a new era.

FASHION

AFTER THE WAR
THE 'NEW LOOK'

As the decade began, the simple, drab, styles from wartime remained as materials were still in short supply and for many this remained the case for several years. However, with the introduction of colour into the country again, in the home and in textiles, fashion for many women returned with a vengeance. The years are known for two silhouettes, that of Christian Dior's 'New Look', the tiny waist, pointy breasts and a full skirt to just below the knee, all achieved with a "waspie" girdle and the pointiest bra seen in history and the pencil slim tubular skirt, also placing emphasis on a narrow waist.

Neat, tailored suits with pencil skirts or fitted dresses, now updated with block colours were the choice for work and by the second half of the decade, the wide circle skirts in colourful cotton prints were in and were worn supported by bouffant net petticoats, stiffened either with conventional starch or a strong sugar solution, to give the right look.

THE *Lift* THAT
NEVER LETS YOU DOWN

Elizabeth Taylor

ALL CHANGE

If a lady was 'formally dressed', she would wear short white cotton gloves for daytime and a decorative hat as a finishing touch. Hairstyles 'for the lady' were stiff, structured and arranged even when worn loose. The permanent wave, in styles worn by the Queen and Elizabeth Taylor, were universally worn, the styling more easily copied with the introduction of hair lacquers and plastic rollers. By 1955 almost 30,000 hair salons had sprung up in Britain.

Grace Kelly epitomised the elegance of the 50s, but there were many who rebelled against the look, including actress Audrey Hepburn who often wore simple black sweaters, flat shoes and short. They gave a continental, chic alternative and had many followers. In 1954, Chanel began to produce boxy classic Chanel suit jackets and slim skirts in braid trimmed, highly textured tweeds. The lines were straight down, losing the nipped in waist and this fashion was easy to copy by major chain stores and very wearable.

IN THE 1950s

THE YOUNG ONES

It was different, the new 'teenager' had their own ideas, girls sported youthful ponytails and were no longer prepared to look like their mothers until they were of age.

The consumer boom arrived with 'teen' clothes becoming available and fashion was influenced by America. Rock 'n' roll idols and film stars set fashions and many boys wanted the black leather and denim jeans look from Brando whilst girls embraced the 'preppie' full dirndl skirts teamed with a scoop neck blouse, back to front cardigan or tight polo neck.

There were the Teddy Boys and Beatniks, but the majority of British male teenagers looked smart. A basic blazer or jacket, with a fashionable narrow tie and even suede shoes.

WEDDING DRESS OF THE DECADE

Grace Kelly and Prince Rainier of Monaco married in 1956. Her dress was designed by Helen Rose, an American who spent the bulk of her career with MGM and was a wedding present from the film studio. It was made from 25 yards of silk taffeta and used antique rose-point lace and pearls.

The fitted bodice was overlaid with lace to the throat, culminating in a small standing collar and closed with a long centre row of tiny buttons. The long sleeves were also lace, and the dress had a full skirt and sweeping train.

The romantic look was completed by the lace and pearl encrusted prayer book the bride carried down the aisle.

WINNING THE POOLS

Football Pools were a 'betting pool' for predicting the outcome of top-level football matches taking place in the coming week. It was typically cheap to play and entries were sent to Littlewoods or Vernons, by post, or collected from your home by agents.

The most popular game was the Treble Chance where you had to predict the matches to end in a 'draw'.

O TWO RESULTS FROM EACH RULED SECTION				
180-1 TEN RESULTS				
South'pton Bury				
Peterboro' Barnsley				
Aldershot Southport				
Bradford C. Barrow				
Brentford Mansfield				
Crewe Al. Gillingham				
York C. Doncaster				
Dunf'mline Raith R.				
Dundee Dundee U.				
Rangers Hibernian				
Bolton W. Fulham				
Everton Sheff. W.				
Leicester Notts F.				
Chelsea Charlton				
Brighton Hull City				
Colchester Coventry				
Millwall Watford				
Chesterf'ld Exeter C.				
Oxford U. Hartlepools				
Torquay U. Lincoln C.				
Arsenal Man. Utd.				
Birmingh'm Leyton O.				
Blackburn Liverpool				
Blackpool Wolves				
Man. City Aston Villa				
Luton T. Rotherham				
Middlesbro' Huddersf'd				
Newcastle Portsmouth				
Walsall Preston				

CORRECT SCOR
DOUBLES · TREBLES · ACCUMULAT

Home	Away	H	A	H	A	H
Sheff. Un.	Ipswich T.					
Grimsby T.	Scunthorpe					
Leeds U.	Sunderland					
Swansea	Stoke C.					
Bristol R.	Crystal P.					
Notts C.	Bourne'mth					

Max.: Doubles £1, Trebles & Accum. S/-, Min. 3d.

SHORT LIST

11-1 THREE HOMES 12-1 THREE AWAYS

W. Brom. Burnley
West Ham Tottenh'm
Derby Co. Cardiff C
Leeds Un. Sunderl'd
Notts Co. Bourne'th
Shrewsb'y Bristol C
Airdrie Kilmarn'k
Falkirk Motherw'l

STAKES

TREBLE

12-1 THREE WINS 20-1 TWO WINS ONE DRAW

W. Brom. Burnley
Notts Co. Bourne'th
Shrewsb'y Bristol C

Britain was almost obsessed with all things American after the war and the first Wimpy Bars opened in Britain in 1954, selling hamburgers, expresso coffee and milkshakes. Named after a fat friend of 'Popeye', the Wimpy bar added the 'British' elements of waitress service and cutlery. They became very popular, especially with the decade's 'new' teenagers who welcomed the addition to the high street's coffee bars and juke boxes.

CAN YOU COME OUT TO PLAY?

Friends would knock on the door straight after breakfast and you would often not come back till tea-time. Streets had little traffic and could be transformed with a couple of pullovers into a football or cricket pitch.

Towns had areas still devastated by bomb damage providing excellent dens and in the country, you could 'go up the woods', ideal for Cowboys and Indians. Those with bikes would cycle for miles, heading for the countryside or city parks to find trees to climb and fall out of, knees always seemed to be grazed and muddy. There were streams to paddle in or fish for stickle backs.

Girls could spend hours skipping or playing hopscotch drawn on the path, whilst their 'babies' slept in the toy prams alongside. Boys playing British bulldog would be rushing past girls, their dresses tucked into the legs of their knickers, practicing handstands against a wall or cartwheels. Saturday night was bath night!

IN THE 1950s

BUTLIN'S HOLIDAY CAMP SKEGNESS
IT'S QUICKER BY RAIL

THE GREAT BRITISH SEASIDE HOLIDAY

The heyday of the great British seaside holiday was in the 1950s and particularly for those living in industrial towns where 'wakes weeks', when the whole factory would shut down and all workers took their annual two weeks holiday at the same time. Convoys of coaches would leave the grime behind, ferrying happy families to the seaside. Blackpool or Scarborough, Brighton or Margate.

The choice was to stay in a guest house or hotel, or for thousands, it was the excitement of a holiday camp such as Butlins or Pontins. Heaven for children, the many activities on offer included the swimming pool, cinema, fairground rides all 'inclusive', no extra charge. Three meals a day were included, served in the communal dining hall and 'Red Coats' at Butlins, or 'Blue Coats' at Pontins, organised daytime activities for both adults and children. Even a 'knobbly knees' and 'gkamourous granny' contests. For the evenings, there was the traditional entertainment, song and dance and comedy shows.

The British seaside resorts provided fun and respite from daily life for the masses, with amusement arcades, candyfloss stalls and seafood shacks selling cockles and whelks in paper cones. Cafes served fish and chips with white bread and butter, accompanied by mugs of tea. There were donkey rides on the sand, roundabouts, helter-skelters and dodgems. On the prom shops sold rock, postcards, buckets and spades and, whatever the weather, families in rented deck chairs sheltered behind windbreaks on the beach, watching the children build sandcastles, play ball and paddle in the sea.

Only the unpredictable British weather could spoil the fun.

1950 The UK singles chart did not exist before 1952 and a song's popularity was measured by the sales of sheet music. This year's top sellers ranged from **You're Breaking My Heart** by Vic Damone, through **Bewitched** by Doris Day to **Rudolph the Red Nosed Reindeer**, the Christmas 'no 1' from Bing Crosby.

1951 **I Taut I Saw a Puddy Tat** was sung by Mel Blanc who was 'the voice' of Tweety and Silvester in the US cartoons. It was the best seller for three weeks, sold over 2m copies and has been recorded by several artists since. Less of a novelty, was **Too Young** by Jimmy Young, who went on to DJ for Radio 2 for almost 30 years.

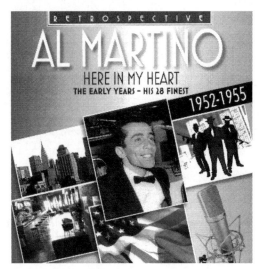

1952 The first 'official' No 1 in the UK, compiled from the best-selling songs by a telephone sample of about 20 shops and published in 'NME' in November was **Here in My Heart** by Al Martino.

1953 Frankie Lane was the singer of the year, **I Believe** topped the charts for 18 non-consecutive weeks and he had 8 top 10 entries, with 2 reaching No 1. Both David Whitfield and Frankie Lane reached a joint top spot, with the same song, at the same time **Answer Me.**

1954 **Secret Love** was Doris Day's second No1 and became the best-selling record of the year. Eddie Calvert, the British trumpeter had a No 1 for 9 weeks, with **Oh Mein Papa.**

1955 Songs seemed to stay at the top longer in the 50's, and Slim Whitmans **Rose Marie** from the musical of the same name, was there for 9 weeks. Tony Bennett made another song from a show, **Stranger in Paradise** from Kismet, a hit too. year but the best-seller was **I'll Be Home** by Pat Boone.

1956 Now, Rock 'n' Roll hit the world! Bill Hayley & his Comets, stormed to No 1 with **Rock Around the Clock** right at the beginning of the year but the best-seller was **I'll Be Home** by Pat Boone.

1957 This was a year for the Brits with hits from Tommy Steele **Singing the Blues**, Frankie Vaughan's **Garden of Eden**, Lonnie Donegan with **Cumberland Gap** and **Gamblin' Man** but the Canadian Paul Anka outsold them with **Diana**.

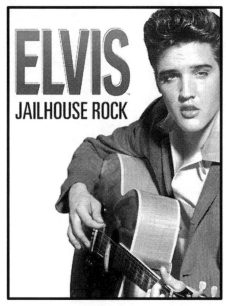

1958 Elvis Presley continued on his way to 21 UK No 1's with **Jailhouse Rock** and the Everly Brothers had the first of their No 1's with **All I Have to Do Is Dream.**

1959 **Living Doll** by Cliff Richard and the Drifters made it to No 1 and later with The Shadows with **Travelling Light**. Adam Faith makes his debut with **What Do You Want.**

In The 1950s

Buddy Holly

During his short career, Holly wrote and recorded many songs. He is often regarded as the artist who defined the traditional rock-and-roll lineup of two guitars, bass, and drums.

That'll Be The Day topped the US "Best Sellers in Stores" chart in September 1957 when they also released **Peggy Sue.**

Buddy Holly (above) and Buddy Holly and the Crickets.(left)

The 50's legend had a huge posthumous hit with **It Doesn't Matter Anymore** and **Raining in My Heart** in 1959, shortly after he was tragically killed in a plane crash in the February. His death was the event later dubbed as "The Day the Music Died" by singer-songwriter Don McLean in his 1971 song **American Pie.**

British Rock and Roll

In the '50s, American rock 'n' roll arrived in Britain, dominated the popular music world and became a huge influence on the newly burgeoning youth culture.

It was a fusion of rhythm and blues, gospel music, country and western and pop. Bill Hayley's '**Rock Around the Clock**', Elvis with '**Hound Dog**' and '**Jailhouse Rock**', Little Richard and Jerry Lee Lewis, inspired British the rock'n'roll groups who emerged from the already popular skiffle groups.

Tommy Steele was one of the first to become a teen idol, with Marty Wilde, Billy Fury and others soon following, but it was Cliff Richard and The Shadows' hit '**Move It**', in 1958, that caused British rock 'n' roll to explode.

Tommy Steele

Cliff Richards and The Shadows

SCIENCE AND NATURE

A DECADE OF INVENTIONS

The 1950s was a period when a plethora of new innovations and inventions were made many still very much in use in the 21st Century. Credit cards, super glue, video tape recorder, oral contraceptives, non-stick Teflon pans, hovercraft, integrating circuit, microchip, transistor radio, heart pacemaker, wireless tv remote, solar panels, polio vaccine, automatic sliding doors, polypropylene, Fortran, the hard disk, power steering and of course, the hula hoop and Barbie dolls.

Black Box Flight Recorder

This invention by an Australian, David Warren, has saved many lives since it was introduced in 1953.

Before then, the cause of most plane crashes, unless there was a surviving pilot, remained unknown, and working as a researcher at an Aeronautical Laboratory in Melbourne, Warren realised that if there was a device in the cockpit that recorded the pilot's voice and read instruments, the information gathered could reveal the cause of the crash and could possibly prevent subsequent ones.

His first device called the Flight Memory Unit could record about four hours of voice and certain parameters but was rejected on grounds of privacy by the Australian aviation community.

Luckily, British officials accepted it, production of the devices in fireproof containers, began and it was taken up by airlines around the world. Some years later it was made compulsory for Australia.

Bar Codes

Joseph Woodland and Bernard Silver invented the first bar code in 1951. At the time Bernard was a graduate at Drexel Institute of Technology, Philadelphia which was contacted by a local food store that wanted a means to automatically read product information when customers checked out.

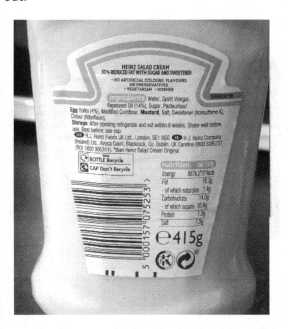

Woodland was at the beach thinking about this when he started drawing random lines in the sand with four of his fingers. He realised he had found one way to solve the food store owner's problem, data could be represented by varying the widths and spacings of parallel lines and thus be able to be read by a machine.

Using UV light sensitive ink he and his colleagues worked on prototypes until they came out with the scannable bar code which has helped make the modern economy.

In The 1950s

Winter of Terror

The Winter of Terror was a three-month period during the winter of 1950–1951 when the Alps were hit by the worst avalanche season ever seen. Thought to be the result of an Atlantic warm front meeting a polar cold front, the destruction mostly affected Austria and Switzerland.

A January snowstorm that lasted two days, added up to four metres of snowfall to a base that was already twice the seasonal average and strong winds caused drifting which led to unstable masses of snow being built up over wide areas. This was to come tumbling down in hundreds of avalanches, burying villages and killing in excess of 200 people.

Thousands of acres of valuable forest were damaged, livestock suffocated, and hundreds of buildings were destroyed. The Swiss town of Andermatt was hit by six avalanches within an hour and 13 people died.

Fifties Floods

1952: In August, the tiny village of Lynmouth, north Devon, suffered the worst river flood in English history. On the 15th, just over 9in (230mm) of rain fell, estimated at 90m tons, over north Devon and west Somerset.

The 1953 Floods in the Netherlands

1953: The great North Sea flood of January caused catastrophic damage and loss of life in Scotland, England, Belgium and The Netherlands and was Britain's worst peacetime disaster on record claiming the lives of 307 people.

In the Netherlands where 50% of the land is less than 1 metre (3.3 ft) above sea level there were 1,836 deaths and widespread damage

1950 The 4th **FIFA World Cup** is held for the first time since 1938 (1942 and 1946 were cancelled during the war). Brazil is the host nation and loses to Uruguay in the finals.

American Joey Maxim wins the light-heavyweight world **Boxing** title, stopping World Champion Freddie Mills of Britain in 10 rounds.

The 4th **British Empire Games** (later called the Commonwealth Games) are held in New Zealand.

1951 Ben Hogan wins the **Masters Tournament** for his 5th major title. He goes on to win the **US Open** title later in the year.

In **First Division football**, Tottenham Hotspur win the 1950/51 title and in the **FA Cup**, Newcastle United beats Blackpool.

1952 At the summer **Olympics** in Helsinki, Finland, Emil Zátopek of Czechoslovakia wins three gold medals. The 5,000m and 10,000m and the third - he decided at the last minute to compete in the first marathon of his life. He was nicknamed the 'Czech Locomotive'.

Rocky Marciano wins the **World Heavyweight Championship** title which he holds until 1956.

1953 Italian Alberto Ascari wins the **F1 Driver's Championship** for the second consecutive time, driving a Ferrari on both occasions.

Ken Rosewall won the **Australian Open** for his first grand slam title at just 18 years of age.

Maureen Connolly (USA) becomes the first woman to win the **Grand Slam** in tennis. The Australian Open, the French Open, Wimbledon and the US Open.

1954 At the **FIFA World Cup** held in Switzerland, Hungary squandered a 2-0 lead over West Germany to lose the final 3-2. Considered to be one of the most disappointing finals matches ever.

In **Athletics**, English runner Roger Bannister becames the first person in history to run one mile in under four minutes.

1955 In US thoroughbred **Horse Racing**, 'Nashua' beats 'Swaps' at Washington Park, 'Swaps' only loss in 9 starts. Nashua's owner-breeder, William Woodward Jr. dreams of owning a Derby winner but is shot dead by his wife before he can send 'Nashua' to England to train.

1956 Lew Hoad wins the **Australian Open** for his first grand slam title. He also wins the **French Open** and **Wimbledon** this year.

In **Cricket**, England off-spinner Jim Laker gains a world record taking 19 wickets in the Test match against Australia at Old Trafford. He takes a total of 46 wickets in the five Tests, a record in an England-Australia series.

1957 Jacques Anquetil of France wins the **Tour de France** for the first of his five times.

In **Football**, Stanley Matthews, 'The Wizard of the Dribble' and 'The Magician' makes his last appearance for England in the match against Denmark in Copenhagen.

1958 Pelé makes his debut at the **FIFA World Cup** in Sweden. Brazil defeats the host in the finals to win the cup.

The plane carrying the **Manchester United football team** crashes at Munich Airport, killing 44 people, including eight Manchester United players.

1959 Maria Bueno of Brazil won the **Wimbledon** Ladies Final at 19 years of age, her first grand slam title. She also won the **US Open** that year.

South African golfer, Gary Player, wins his first major title at **The Open** Championship.

The **Rugby** Five Nations Championship is won by France, the team's first outright championship title.

Swimming the English Channel

On 8th August 1950, Florence Chadwick, 'Queen of the Channel', set a new Women's record for swimming the 21 miles of the English Channel from France to England, in 13 hrs 20 mins.

Florence was a typist and swimming coach from California and achieved four successes in her ten attempts. In 1951 she became the first ever woman, at 32 years old, to swim from England to France, which also made her the first woman to ever swim the 'double'.

She made three England to France swims and each one took the record for the fastest time, going from 16 hrs 22 mins in 1951 to 13 hrs 55 mins in 1955. On her last three successful swims she also attempted to swim there-and-back but gave up on the return legs.

The first woman to ever swim the Channel was also an American, Gertrude Ederle, who in 1926, achieved a time of 14 hrs and 34 mins.

The first person to successfully cross the stretch of water was Captain Matthew Webb, who swam the distance in 1875 at his second attempt and took 21 hrs 45 mins.

Juan Manuel Fangio

In May 1950, the Formula One world championship era began, at Silverstone with Alfa Romeo becoming its first super-power, sweeping to victory at the start of the season and remaining unbeaten until the end. The Argentinian driver, a stocky, balding Argentine already in his 40s and nicknamed, 'El Chueco', the 'bowlegged or bandy legged one', dominated the first decade of Formula One, winning the World Driver's Championship five times. He raced for four different teams, Alfa Romeo, Ferrari, Mercedes-Benz and Maserati, winning 24 of his 52 F1 races, including his 'home' Grand Prix in Argentina four times.

At this time F1 cars were fast and physically demanding to drive, races were long and by the end of a GP, drivers often suffered blistered hands from the heavy steering and gear changing and their faces were sometimes covered in soot from the inboard brakes. In 1955, Fangio was teamed with a 25-year-old 'apprentice', Stirling Moss, Britain's brightest prospect.

TRANSPORT

By 1950, Britain was the world's biggest car exporter and most cars on our roads were built in Britain. Here are some of the famous cars.

Ford Popular

When launched in 1953, the Ford Popular was the cheapest car in Britain. But while robust and reliable, it was quite basic; even sun visors cost extra.

Vauxhall Cresta

While Vauxhall's Cresta brought a touch of chrome-clad American glamour to British roads in the 1950s these large cars often succumbed to rust. More than 300,000 were built in Luton from 1948 to 1965.

The Last Steam Trains

Great Britain was the first nation to use steam locomotives and Britain's railway is the oldest in the world but by 1955, a modernisation programme started to replace this vital cog of the nineteenth century industrial revolution with diesel and electric trains.

Morris Minor

More than 1.6 million of this design classic were manufactured and the Minor Series II and Minor 1000 belong to the 1950s.

The Mini

The Mini may be the greatest British classic car of all time. In 1959, Sir Alec Issigonis created a vehicle where passengers used 80% of its interior space. The Mini became an iconic, affordable, family car.

Jaguar XK140

A beautiful sports car with a sleek bonnet and sparkling wheels

In The 1950s

Britain's First Motorway

In December 1958, Prime Minister Harold Macmillan opened the Preston Bypass, the first ever section of motorway in Great Britain, planned as part of a larger scheme to build a north-south motorway network.

Nearly £3 million was spent on the construction of this original 8 ¼ mile, dual two lane, motorway after early work was hampered by foul weather and heavy rainfall which resulted in the postponement of various heavy engineering works. Ultimately, this meant the initial two-year plan was delayed by a further five months.

The following year, the first section of the M1 motorway was opened in November 1959 and with it, the first service station at Watford Gap. Initially there was no speed limit on the motorway and, over three lanes, it gave motorists the chance to drive 50 miles from St Albans to Rugby as fast as their car could manage. The design team anticipated that the road would cope with about 14,000 vehicles each day.

The De Havilland Comet

On 2nd May 1952, the Comet 1 airliner carried passengers on a scheduled commercial route for the very first time. The journey from London to Johannesburg was reportedly a sublimely smooth one. This new aircraft could carry 36 passengers, those in first class sat around tables, at a cruising speed of 450 mph – and a top speed of 503 mph - over a distance of 2,500 miles and BOAC's fleet was the envy of world airlines.

Despite the aim to provide affordable widespread travel in an age where air travel was still the preserve of the rich, the Comet attracted its fair share of highly esteemed passengers. Queen Elizabeth, Princess Margaret and the Queen Mother were all guests of Sir Geoffrey and Lady de Havilland on a special flight in June 1953 and became the first members of the Royal Family to fly by jet.

The advent of passenger jets transformed air travel. Between 1950 and 1960 the number of air passengers carried in the UK increased from just over one million to six million.

THE MAJOR NEWS STORIES

1960

May: Princess Margaret marries photographer, Anthony Armstrong-Jones at Westminster Abbey. It is the first royal marriage to be televised.

Nov: "Lady Chatterley's Lover" sells 200,000 copies in one day following its publication since the ban enforced in 1928 is lifted.

1961

Jan: The farthing, used since the 13th Century, ceases to be legal tender in the UK.

Apr: The US attack on "The Bay of Pigs" in Cuba was defeated within two days by Cuban forces under the direct command of their Premier, Fidel Castro.

1962

Jan: An outbreak of smallpox infects 45 and kills 19 in South Wales. 900,000 people in the region are vaccinated against the disease.

Dec: The "Big Freeze" starts in Britain. There are no frost-free nights until 5 March 1963.

1963

June: Kennedy: 'Ich bin ein Berliner' The US President Kennedy, has made a ground-breaking speech in Berlin offering American solidarity to the citizens of West Germany.

Aug: 'The Great Train Robbery' on the travelling Post Office train from Glasgow to Euston, takes place in Buckinghamshire.

1964

Mar: Radio Caroline, the 'pirate radio station' begins regular broadcasting from a ship just outside UK territorial waters off Felixstowe, Suffolk.

Oct: After thirteen years in power, the Conservatives are beaten by Labour at the General Election and Harold Wilson becomes Prime Minister.

The Tiller Girls At The London Palladium

1962: In April, the five-month-old strike by Equity, the actors' union, against the Independent television companies, ends, with actors gaining huge increases in basic pay rates.

1963: John F. Kennedy, the 35th president of the United States, was assassinated on November 22 in Dallas, Texas, while riding in a presidential motorcade. He was with his wife Jacqueline, Texas Governor John Connally, and Connally's wife Nellie when he was fatally shot from a nearby building by Lee Harvey Oswald. Governor Connally was seriously wounded in the attack. The motorcade rushed to the local hospital, where Kennedy was pronounced dead about 30 minutes after the shooting. Mr Connally recovered.

1969 APOLLO 11. Neil Armstrong becomes the first man to walk on the moon. "One small step for man, one giant leap for mankind."

1965: In January, Sir Winston Churchill dies aged 90. Sir Winston served as Prime Minister of the United Kingdom from 1940-45 and again from 1951-1955. He is best known for his wartime leadership as PM.

1965

Mar: 3,500 US Marines, the first American ground combat troops arrive in Da Nang, South Vietnam.

Aug: Elizabeth Lane is appointed as the first ever female High Court Judge. She is assigned to the Family Division.

1966

Jun: The first British credit card, the Barclaycard, is introduced by Barclays. It has a monopoly in the market until the Access Card is introduced in 1972.

Sept: HMS Resolution is launched at Barrow-in-Furness. It is the first of the Polaris ballistic missile submarines, armed with 16 Polaris A missiles.

1967

Jan: Donald Campbell, the racing driver and speedboat racer, was killed on Coniston Water whilst attempting to break his own speed record.

Dec: The Anglo-French Concorde supersonic aircraft was unveiled in Toulouse, France.

1968

Jun: The National Health Service reintroduces prescription charges, abolished by the Labour Govt. in 1965, at 2s 6d.

Sep: The General Post Office divides their single rate postal service into two. First-class letters at 5d and second-class at 4d.

1969

Mar: The Queen opens the Victoria Line on the London Underground. It is the first entirely new Underground line in London for 50 years.

Dec: The abolition of the death penalty for murder, having been suspended since 1965, was made permanent by Parliament.

At the beginning of the decade, the wireless was still the usual form of entertainment in the home and children could sit comfortably to "Listen with Mother" on the Light Programme and mother could carry on listening to "Woman's Hour" afterwards.

However, television was becoming increasingly affordable, and the two channels, BBC and ITV were joined in 1965 by BBC2. Dr Finlay's Casebook; The Black and White Minstrel Show; Top of the Pops; Perry Mason and Z Cars were the most popular shows of the 60's.

In 1962 the BBC bravely introduced a new satirical show, "That Was the Week That Was" which proved a big hit and by 1969, the BBC was converting programmes to colour.

Children's pocket money, probably 6d (2.5p) a week in the early years, could buy sweets. Black Jacks and Fruit Salads (4 for a penny (0.5p)), sweet cigarettes, lemonade crystals, gob stoppers, flying saucers or toffees, weighed by the shopkeeper in 2oz or 4oz paper bags. All could be eaten whilst reading a copy of The Beano or Dandy, Bunty or Jack and Jill comics.

The simple, yet addictive party game Twister was introduced in 1966.

In the 60's the nuclear family was still the norm, father out at work and mother busy with the housework which was time consuming before the general possession of electrical labour-saving devices.

Washing up was done by hand and laundry gradually moved to machines over the decade.

Twin tubs, one for washing and one for Spinning, became popular in the late 60's and were usually wheeled into the kitchen to be attached to the cold tap and afterwards, have the waste-water emptied into the sink. The 'housewife' had to be at home to transfer the wet washing from the washing tub to the spinning tub.

By the end of the 60's, 58% of households had a small refrigerator but no fridge/freezers, so shopping was still done regularly and, typically, meals were home cooked.

Chicken was expensive but beef was cheaper and olive oil came only in tiny bottles from the chemist to help clean your ears!

In Britain, the domestic freezer is still a luxury but by the mid 60's, some 700m fish fingers were among the 60,000 tons of frozen fish consumed with peas from 35,000 acres and 120,000 quick-frozen chickens.

I spy Birds Eye - the freshest VEGETABLES you can buy!

Goods came to you. The milkman delivered the milk to your doorstep, the baker brought the baskets of bread to the door, the greengrocer delivered and the 'pop man' came once a week with 'dandelion and burdock', 'cherryade' or 'cream soda' and the rag and bone man called down the street for your recycling.

ART AND CULTURE

1960 - 1963

1960 Frederick Ashton's 'La Fille Mal Gardée' premieres by The Royal Ballet at the Royal Opera House.
In court, Penguin Books who published 'Lady Chatterley's Lover' by DH Lawrence, is found not guilty of obscenity.

1961 The 'Betting & Gaming Act' comes into force which allows the operating of commercial Bingo halls.
'Ken' is introduced in the US as a boyfriend for 'Barbie'.

1962 Margot Fonteyn and Rudolf Nureyev first dance together in a Royal Ballet performance of Giselle, in London.
Dec John Steinbeck, American author is awarded the Nobel Prize in Literature. Aleksandr Solzhenitsyn's novella, "One Day in the Life of Ivan Denisovich" is published in Russia.

1963 The first Leeds Piano Competition is held, and Michael Roll is the winner.
Authors CS Lewis and Aldous Huxley both die on 23 November, but news of their deaths is overshadowed by the assassination of JFK.

Margot Fonteyn and Rudolf Nureyev performing The Sleeping Beauty.

Their partnership has been described as the greatest of all time.

1964 - 1969

1964 BBC television airs the first 'Top of the Pops'. Dusty Springfield is the very first artist to perform, with 'I Only Want to Be With You'.
Ernest Hemingway's memoirs of his years in Paris, 'A Moveable Feast' is published posthumously by his wife.

1965 Rembrandt's painting 'Titus' is sold at Christie's London fetching the then record price of 760,000 guineas. (£798,000).
The f*** word is spoken for the first time on television by Kenneth Tynan and two weeks later, Mary Whitehouse founds The National Viewers' and Listeners' Association.

1966 'Rosencrantz and Guildenstern Are Dead' by Tom Stoppard has its debut at the Edinburgh Festival Fringe.
BBC1 televises 'Cathy Come Home', a docudrama that is viewed by a quarter of the British public and goes on to influence attitudes to homelessness.

1967 **'The Summer of Love'.** Thousands of young 'flower children' descend on the west coast of America, for hippie music, hallucinogenic drugs, spiritual meditation and free-love.
BBC radio restructures. The Home Service becomes Radio 4, the Third Programme becomes Radio 3 and the Light Programme is split between Radio 1 (to compete with pirate radio) and Radio 2.

1968 The BBC repeat of the twenty-six episodes of 'The Forsyte Saga' on Sunday evening television, leads to reports of 'publicans and vicars complaining it was driving away their customers and worshippers, respectively' and of 'Evensong services being moved to avoid a clash'.

1969 The Beatles perform together for the last time on the rooftop of Apple Records in London. The impromptu concert was broken up by the police.

IN THE 1960s

The three-day Woodstock Music Festival was held in August 1969 on a dairy farm in Bethel, New York. Nearly half a million young people arrived for "An Aquarian Experience: 3 Days of Peace and Music." Now known simply as Woodstock, the festival was a huge success, but it did not go off without a hitch. The almost 500,000 people who turned up was unexpected and caused the organisers a headache which necessitated venue changes and this was before the bad weather, muddy conditions, lack of food and unsanitary conditions made life even more difficult.

Surprisingly, the event passed off peacefully, this fact attributed by most, to the amount of sex, psychedelic drugs and rock 'n roll that took place. Others say, couples were too busy 'making love not war' to cause trouble, either way, Woodstock earned its place in the halls of pop culture history fame.

"American artist Andy Warhol premieres his "Campbell's Soup Cans" exhibit in Los Angeles".

Andy Warhol famously borrowed familiar icons from everyday life and the media, among them celebrity and tabloid news photos, comic strips, and, in this work, the popular canned soup made by the Campbell's Soup Company. When he first exhibited "Campbell's Soup Cans", the images were displayed together on shelves, like products in a grocery aisle. At the time, Campbell's sold 32 soup varieties and each one of Warhol's 32 canvases corresponds to a different flavour, each having a different label. The first flavour, introduced in 1897, was tomato.

Each canvas was hand painted and the fleur de lys pattern round each can's bottom edge was hand stamped. Warhol said, "I used to drink Campbell's Soup. I used to have the same lunch every day, for 20 years, I guess!"

FILMS

1960 - 1963

1960   Ben Hur, the religious epic, was a remake of a 1925 silent film with a similar title and had the largest budget ($15.175m) and the largest sets built of any film produced at the time.

1961   Billy Wilder's risqué tragi-comedy **The Apartment** won the Academy Award for Best Picture. Starring Jack Lemmon and Shirley MacLaine, it tells a story of an ambitious, lonely insurance clerk who lends out his New York apartment to executives for their love affairs.

1962   New Films released this year included, **Lolita** starring James Mason and Sue Lyon. **Dr No**, the first James Bond film, starring Sean Connery and Ursula Andress and **What Ever Happened to Baby Jane?** a horror film with Bette Davis

1963   Lawrence of Arabia, based on author TS Eliot's book 'Seven Pillars of Wisdom' and starring Peter O'Toole and Alec Guinness won the Oscar for Best Picture.
The publicity of the affair between the stars, Elizabeth Taylor and Richard Burton, helped make **Cleopatra** a huge box office success but the enormous production costs, caused the film to be a financial disaster.

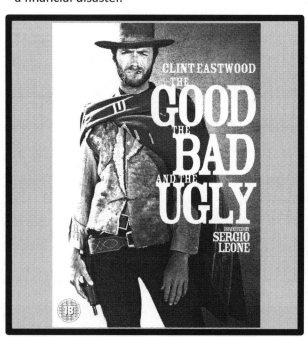

1964 - 1969

1964   The historical adventure, sex comedy romp **Tom Jones** won four Oscars, Best Picture, Best Director, Best Adapted Screenplay and Best Musical Score. Albert Finney starred as the titular hero and Susannah York as the girl he loves.

1965   Winning the Oscar this year, the film **My Fair Lady,** based on George Bernard Shaw's play 'Pygmalion', tells the story of Eliza Doolittle and her quest to 'speak proper' in order to be presentable in Edwardian London's high society. Rex Harrison and Audrey Hepburn starred and it became the 2nd highest grossing film of the year just behind **The Sound of Music** which won the Academy Award the following year.

1966   The Good, the Bad and the Ugly was directed by Sergio Leonie, the Italian director who gave rise to the term 'spaghetti western'- a genre of westerns produced and directed by Italians. Clint Eastwood was the Good, Lee Van Cleef, the Bad and Eli Wallach, the Ugly. The film was a huge success and catapulted Clint Eastwood to fame.

1967   The fun filled seduction of Benjamin Braddock by Mrs Robinson in **The Graduate** made the film the biggest grossing production of the year world-wide.

1968   The famous quote "They call me Mister Tibbs" comes from **In the Heat of the Night** where Sidney Poitier plays Virgil Tibbs, a black police detective from Philadelphia, caught up in a murder investigation in racially hostile Mississippi. Rod Steiger is the white chief of police.

1969   Oliver the musical based on Dicken's novel and Lionel Bart's stage show, carried off the Oscar for Best Picture.

Editor's Note: The Academy Awards are held in February and each year's awards are presented for films that were first shown during the full preceding calendar year from January 1 to December 31 Los Angelis, California. Source: Wikipedia

THE FIRST JAMES BOND FILM!

HARRY SALTZMAN and ALBERT R. BROCCOLI PRESENT IAN FLEMING'S

DR. NO

TECHNICOLOR

SEAN CONNERY AS 007 · URSULA ANDRESS · JOSEPH WISEMAN · JACK LOI

This was the first-ever launch of a James Bond film in a cinema and was attended by the stars, Sean Connery and Ursula Andress together with the James Bond creator Ian Fleming. The plot of this British spy film revolves around James Bond who needs to solve the mystery of the strange disappearance of a British agent to Jamaica and finds an underground base belonging to Dr No who is plotting to disrupt the American space launch with a radio beam weapon. The film was condemned by The Vatican as "a dangerous mixture of violence, vulgarity, sadism, and sex".

1962 : "West Side Story" Wins The Academy Awards "Best Picture" category.

The musical with lyrics by Stephen Sondheim and music by Leonard Bernstein was inspired by the story of William Shakespeare's "Romeo and Juliet". Set in the mid 1950s in Upper West Side of New York City, which was then, a cosmopolitan working-class area, it follows the rivalry between the Jets and the Sharks, two teenage street gangs from different ethnic backgrounds.

The Sharks are from Puerto Rico and are taunted by the white Jets gang. The hero, Tony, a former member of the Jets falls in love with Maria, the sister of the leader of the Sharks. The sophisticated music and the extended dance scenes, focussing on the social problems marked a turning point in musical theatre. The film starred Natalie Wood and Richard Beymer.

FASHION

CHANGING FASHION

It was a decade of three parts for fashion. The first years were reminiscent of the fifties, conservative and restrained, classic in style and design. Jackie Kennedy, the President's glamorous wife, was very influential with her tailored suit dresses and pill box hats, white pearls and kitten heels.

The hairdresser was of extreme importance. Beehive coiffures worn by the likes of Dusty Springfield and Brigitte Bardot were imitated by women of all ages and Audrey Hepburn popularised the high bosom, sleeveless dress. Whilst low, square toed shoes were high fashion, 'on the street', stilettos rivalled them.

THE MODS

In the mid-60s, the look had become sleeker and more modern. The lines were form-fitting but didn't try to accentuate curves. There were brighter colours and for the young, the Mod style.

Male mods took on a smooth, sophisticated look that included tailor-made suits with narrow lapels, thin ties, button-down collar shirts and wool jumpers.

The pea coat and Chelsea boots looked very 'London'. The Beatles were leading the way, hair started to grow longer, and trousers lost the baggy, comfortable fit of the 1950's.

For girls, shift dresses and mini skirts became shorter and shorter, worn with flat shoes or 'go go boots', short hair with eyebrow brushing fringes, and little makeup, just a pale lipstick and false eyelashes.

Slender models like Jean Shrimpton and Twiggy exemplified the look and new, exciting designers emerged such as Mary Quant. Television shows like 'Ready Steady Go!' showed their audiences at home, what they should be wearing.

IN THE 1960s

THE HIPPIES

For the young, jeans were becoming ubiquitous both for men and women, skin-tight drainpipes through to the flared bottoms of the late years. London had taken over from Paris to become the fashion centre of the world and in contrast to the beginning of the decade, the end was the exact opposite.

Bright, swirling colours. Psychedelic, tie-dye shirts, long hair and beards were commonplace. Individualism was the word and mini skirts were worn alongside brightly coloured and patterned tunics with flowing long skirts.

CARNABY STREET

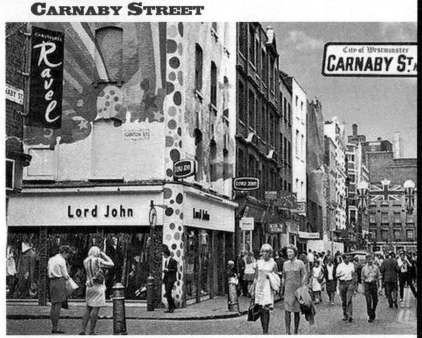

By 1967, Carnaby Street was popular with followers of the mod and hippie styles. Many fashion designers, such as Mary Quant, Lord John and Irvine Sellars, had premises there, and underground music bars, such as the Roaring Twenties, opened in the surrounding streets.

Bands such as the Small Faces, The Who and The Rolling Stones appeared in the area, to work at the legendary Marquee Club round the corner in Wardour Street, to shop, and to socialise. The Street became one of the coolest destinations associated with 1960s Swinging London.

LEISURE

THE PACKAGE HOLIDAY

By the mid-sixties, the traditional British seaside holiday, sandcastles, donkey rides, sticks of rock and fish and chips on the beach was gradually giving way to the new and exciting Package Holiday in the sun.

Tour operators began taking plane loads of holidaymakers abroad, almost exclusively to Europe and to Spain in particular. Hotels were springing up everywhere, often obscuring the 'exotic views' that the tourists were promised and were basic with rather simple local fare, which even then was not to the taste of a large majority. Restaurants flourished with 'Full English Breakfast' posters displayed all over the windows, tea and beer were in demand.

By the end of the decade, Luton Airport, a favourite with the tour firms, had flights arriving back every hour full of sunburnt Brits wearing sombreros and clutching Spanish donkeys and maracas.

A cold British beach holiday was replaced for many by cheap package holidays to sunny Spain.

"LET'S GO FOR A CHINESE"

A 'Greasy Spoon'

A cheese-pineapple hedgehog

In the early 1960s, eating out was expensive and apart from 'greasy spoon' cafes, or a packet of salted crisps at a pub, dining out was limited to formal restaurants. However, with a rise in immigrants from Asia, Chinese and Indian restaurants were springing up and their relatively affordable and tasty food became so popular that Vesta brought out their first 'foreign convenience' foods, the Vesta Curries and Vesta Chow Mein.

A cheaper alternative was inviting friends to eat at home, and the dinner party boomed from the end of the decade. Pre-dinner drinks were often served with cubes of tinned pineapple and cheddar cheese on sticks, stuck into half a tinfoil covered grapefruit to look like a hedgehog – the height of 60s sophistication! The main course might feature the fashionable 'spaghetti bolognese', and 'Blue Nun', Mateus Rosé or Chianti wine, adding a hint of sophistication to the new 'smart' set's evening.

Teenage Leisure

The 60's became the era for the teenager, but it started off with the same disciplines as the fifties. At school the teachers commanded respect and gave out punishment when it was not given. Parents could determine when and where their children could be out of house, gave sons and daughters chores to do and families ate together and watched television together.

Scouts and Guides were still very popular and a natural progression from the years as Cubs and Brownies and Outward Bounding or working for the Duke of Edinburgh Awards remained popular for many, but as the decade wore on, the lure of the new found freedom for the young was hard for many to overcome. Coffee bars became the place to meet, drink coffee or chocolate, listen to the latest hits on the juke box and talk with friends. The political climate influenced them, they demonstrated in the streets against the Vietnam War, for civil rights and to 'Ban the Bomb'. They developed the 'hippie' point of view, advocating non-violence and love, and by the end of the decade, "Make Love not War" was the 'flower children's' mantra.

Outdoor music festivals sprang up all over the country and thousands of, usually mud-caked, teenagers gathered to listen to their favourite artists, rock concerts played to packed houses and the young experimented with marijuana and LSD. Psychedelic art was incorporated into films, epitomised by the Beatles' 'Yellow Submarine'.

1960 **Poor Me by Adam Faith**, a teen idol, reached number 1 and stayed there for two weeks whilst his previous number 1 hit, **What Do You Want** was still in the top ten. The Everly Brothers, the American rock duo, had their fifth number 1 with **Cathy's Clown**. Their first was Bye Bye Love in 1957. A surprise number 1 for four weeks was by Lonnie Donnegan, the skiffle singer, with **My Old Man's a Dustman.**

1961 **Wooden Heart** sung by Elvis Presley stayed at number 1 for six weeks and became the best-selling UK single of the year. Johnny Leyton had a three-week number 1 with **Johnny Remember Me** in August and it returned to the number 1 spot again at the end of September. Teenage singer and actress Helen Shapiro, had her second number one, **Walkin' Back to Happiness**, whilst still only fifteen.

1962 The top selling single of the year was by the Australian singer, Frank Ifield. **I Remember You** was sung in a yodelling, country-music style.

Acker Bilk's **Stranger on the Shore** becomes the first British recording to reach the number 1 spot on the US Billboard Hot 100.

The Rolling Stones make their debut at London's Marquee Club, opening for Long John Baldry.

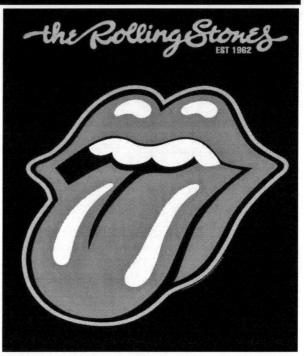

1962: The Rolling Stones make their debut at London's Marquee Club playing the rock n' roll of Chuck Berry and Bo Diddley.

1963 The Beatles have three number 1's in the UK charts in their first year. **From Me to You**, **She Loves You** and **I Want to Hold Your Hand.** Their debut album, **Please Please Me**, reaches the top of the album charts.

Produced by Phil Spector, The Crystals have a hit with **And Then He Kissed Me**

How Do You Do What You Do to Me, the debut single by Liverpudlian band Gerry and the Pacemakers, stays at number 1 for three weeks in April.

1964 The Hollies, the Merseybeat group founded by school friends Allan Clarke and Graham Nash, reach number 2 in the UK charts with **Just One Look**, a cover of the song by Doris Troy in the US.

Originally written by Burt Bacharach for Dionne Warwick, **Anyone Who Had a** Heart, sung by Cilla Black, became a UK number 1 for three weeks and was also the fourth best-selling single of 1964 in the UK, with sales of around 950,000 copies.

"The Fab Four", John Lennon, Paul McCartney, George Harrison and Ringo Star were the ultimate pop phenomenon of the '60s.

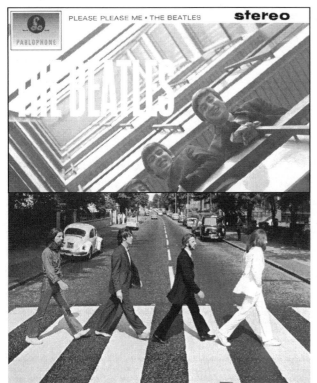

IN THE 1960s

1965 Unchained Melody by The Righteous Brothers, with a solo by Bobby Hatfield becomes a jukebox standard. **Its Not Unusual** sung by Tom Jones becomes an international hit after being promoted by the offshore, pirate radio station, Radio Caroline. **Get Off of My Cloud** by The Rolling Stones was written by Mick Jagger and Keith Richards as a single to follow their previous hit of the year, **(I Can't Get No) Satisfaction**.

1966 Nancy Sinatra with **These Boots Are Made for Walkin'** reaches number 1.
Good Vibrations sung by The Beach Boys, becomes an immediate hit both sides of the Atlantic.
Ike and Tina Turner released **River Deep, Mountain High** and their popularity soars in the UK after a tour with The Rolling Stones.

1967 Waterloo Sunset by The Kinks, written by Ray Davies, reached number 2 in the British charts and was a top 10 hit in Australia, New Zealand and most of Europe. In North America, it failed to chart.
A Whiter Shade of Pale the debut single by Procul Harem stays at number 1 for eight weeks.
Sandie Shaw wins the Eurovision Song Contest with **Puppet on a String**.

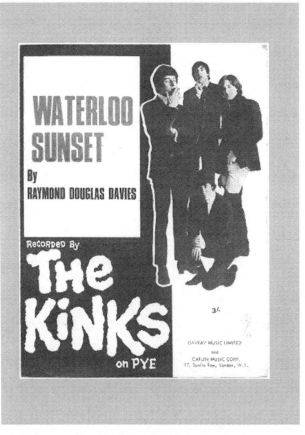

1968 Dusty Springfield's **Son of a Preacher Man** was her last top thirty hit until her collaboration with The Pet Shop Boys in 1987. In 1994, **Preacher Man** was included in Tarantino's film 'Pulp Fiction'.
Manfred Mann has a resounding success with **Mighty Quinn**, their third UK number 1 and third hit singing a song written by Bob Dylan.
The comedy group The Scaffold's record, **Lily the Pink** released in November became number 1 for the four weeks over the Christmas holidays.

1969 Where Do You Go To (My Lovely)? by the British singer-songwriter Peter Sarstedt stayed at number 1 for four weeks.
I Heard It Through the Grapevine was written in 1966 and recorded by Gladys Knight and the Pips. However, it was the version by Marvin Gaye that took the number 1 spot in the UK for three weeks and became the biggest hit single on the Motown label.
Je t'aime… moi non plus was written in 1967 for Brigitte Bardot but Serge Gainsbourg and Jane Birkin recorded the best known version and the duet reached number 1 in the UK. It was banned in several countries due to its overtly sexual content.

SCIENCE AND NATURE

THE LONDON SMOG

Britain still experienced "pea-soupers" in the 60's and in December 1962, London suffered under a choking blanket of smog. After three days, the noxious layer spread all over the country.

Smog is a concentration of smoke particles and other substances such as sulphur dioxide, combined with fog in conditions of low temperature, high pressure and lack of wind. Visibility was reduced such that a light could only be seen at 50ft and in spite of people covering their faces with scarves, surgical masks or handkerchiefs, the overwhelming smell of sulphur and coal smoke left an unpleasant metallic taste in the mouth and irritated eyes and noses. Bronchitis increased significantly and it is estimated that, in Greater London alone, there were 700 deaths in total.

In 1962, the Duke of Edinburgh was in New York for the inaugural dinner of the US branch of the World Wildlife Fund, first set up in Zurich in 1961, and warned his audience that our descendants could be forced to live in a world where the only living creature would be man himself -"*always assuming,*" he said, "*that we don't destroy ourselves as well in the meantime.*"

In his speech, the Duke described poachers who were threatening extermination of many big game animals in Africa as "killers for profit ... the get-rich-at-any-price mob." African poachers, he said, were killing off the rhinoceros to get its horn for export to China, "*where, for some incomprehensible reason, they seem to think it acts as an aphrodisiac.*" The Duke also criticised the status seekers – people "like the eagle chasers". The bald eagle in North America was being chased and killed by people in light aeroplanes who seem to think it smart to own its feathers and claws.

"*What is needed, above all now,*" he said, "*are people all over the world who understand the problem and really care about it. People who have the courage to see that the conservation laws are obeyed.*"

DUKE OF EDINBURGH LAUNCHES WORLD WILDLIFE FUND

IN THE 1960s

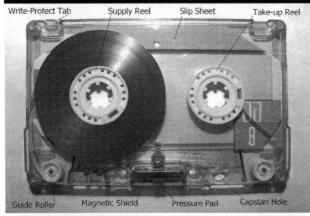

Write-Protect Tab Supply Reel Slip Sheet Take-up Reel

Guide Roller Magnetic Shield Pressure Pad Capstan Hole

THE CASSETTE TAPE

The cassette tape was first developed by Philips in Belgium in 1962. These two small spools inside its plastic case, which wind magnetic-coated film on which the audio content is stored and pass it from one side to the other, meant music could now be recorded and shared by everyone.

Up until now, music was typically recorded on vinyl which needed a record player, or on reel-to-reel recorders which were comparatively expensive and difficult to use and neither of which were portable. The cassette player allowed individuals to record their favourite songs easily and also take their music with them "on-the-go". Music lovers soon learned how to create their own mixed tapes, for themselves or to share with friends.

More than 3 billion tapes were sold between 1962 and 1988.

THE ABERFAN DISASTER

On 21 October 1966, the worst mining-related disaster in British history took place in Aberfan, in South Wales. Coal was mined there for domestic heating and the waste was dumped at the top of the valley on land of no economic value. But crucially, it was tipped on highly porous sandstone which overlaid at least one natural spring.

During October 1966 heavy rainfall led to a build-up of water within this tip and caused it to collapse. With a deafening roar, 107 cu m of black slurry turned into an avalanche. The deluge leapt over the old railway embankment into the village where destroyed 18 houses and Pant Glas Junior School together with part of the neighbouring County Secondary School.

In total, 144 lives were lost, 116 of them children, 109 of these were aged between seven and ten and died in their classrooms on the last day before half term. Of the 28 adults who died, five were primary school teachers.

The official inquiry placed the blame entirely on the National Coal Board.

1960 - 1969

1960   In tennis, Rod Laver wins his first grand slam title as a 21-year-old taking the **Australian Open.**
Jack Brabham wins the **F1 driver's championship** for the second straight time.

1961   **Five Nations Championship** (now 6 Nations) rugby series is won by France.
Tottenham Hotspur beat Leicester City 2-0 in the **FA Cup Final.**

1962   Sonny Liston knocks out Floyd Pattison after two minutes into the first round of the "Boxing World Title" fight in Chicago.

1963   Mill House, at 18 hands, known as 'The Big Horse', wins the **Cheltenham Gold Cup.**

1964   The **Tour de France i**s won by Jacques Anquetil of France, the first cyclist to win the Tour five times. 1957 and 1961-64.

1965   At the **Masters** in Atlanta, Jack Nicklaus shoots a record 17 under par to win the tournament.
In the **FA Cup Final** at Wembley, Liverpool beats Leeds United 2-1.

1966   England defeat Germany to win the **FIFA World Cup**

1967   Defending champion Billie Jean King defeats Ann Haydon-Jones in the **Wimbledon Women's Singles Championship**.
The New York Yacht Club retains the **America's Cup** when 'Intrepid' beat the Australian challenger 'Dame Pattie', 4 races to 1.

1968   English International cricketer Basil D'Oliveira, of 'Cape Coloured' background, is excluded from the **MCC South African tour** side, leading to turmoil in the world of cricket.

1969   **The Grand National i**s won by 12-year-old Highland Wedding by 12 lengths.

1966 FIFA World Cup

On July 30th, England and West Germany lined up at Wembley to determine the winner of the 'Jules Rimet Trophy', the prize for winning the World Cup. England won 4-2 after extra time and the match is remembered for Geoff Hurst's hat-trick and the controversial third goal awarded to England by the referee and linesman.

In addition to an attendance of 96,924 at the stadium, the British television audience peaked at 32.3 million viewers, making it the UK's most-watched television event ever.

It was the first occasion that England had hosted, or won, the World Cup and was to remain their only major tournament win. It was also the nation's last final at a major international football tournament for 55 years, until 2021 when England reached the Euro Final but lost to Italy after a penalty shootout.

IN THE 1960s

1964 OLYMPIC GAMES

In 1964, the first Olympic Games to be held in Asia, took place in Japan during October to avoid the city's midsummer heat and humidity and the September typhoon season. It marked many milestones in the history of the modern Games; a cinder running track was used for the last time in the athletics events, whilst a fibreglass pole was used for the first time in the pole-vaulting competition. These Games were also the last occasion that hand timing by stopwatch was used for official timing.

25 world records were broken and 52 of a possible 61 Olympic records were also broken. Ethiopian runner Abebe Bikila won his second consecutive Olympic marathon. Bob Hayes won the men's 100 metres and then anchored the US 400 metre relay team to a world record victory. Peter Snell, the New Zealand middle-distance runner, won both the 800 and 1500 metres, the only man to have done so in the same Olympics since 1920. Ann Packer of Britain made a record-breaking debut winning gold in the 800 metres and silver in the 400 metres.

Peter Snell, winning the 1500 metres.

CASSIUS CLAY HEAVYWEIGHT CHAMPION OF THE WORLD

In 1964, Cassius Clay, later this year to be known as Muhammad Ali, fought and gained Sonny Liston's title of Heavyweight Champion of the World. The big fight took place in Miami Beach in February.

Liston was an intimidating fighter and Clay was the 7-1 under-dog, but still he engaged in taunting his opponent during the build-up to the fight, dubbing him *"the big ugly bear"*, stating *"Liston even smells like a bear"* and claiming, *"After I beat him, I'm going to donate him to the zoo!"*
The result of the fight was a major upset as Clay's speed and mobility kept him out of trouble and in the third round hit Liston with a combination that opened a cut under his left eye and eventually, Liston could not come out for the seventh round.
A triumphant Clay rushed to the edge of the ring and, pointing to the ringside press, shouted: *"Eat your words!"* adding the words he was to live up to for the rest of his life, *"I am the greatest!"*

TRANSPORT

Trolleybuses were taken out of service in London in May having served since 1931.

How luxurious can an Austin Seven get?

The revolutionary Mini was the fastest selling small car in Britain in the 60s. Despite the promise of the adverts early models were slow and unreliable and although promoted as a luxury family car, it was uncomfortable and cramped.

THE VICKERS VC10

The 60's produced Britain's biggest airliner to date, the four jet Vickers VC10. With a towering tailplane, high as a four-storey house, the airliner weighed 150 tons fully loaded and was 158ft long. In service with BOAC and other airlines from the end of 1963 until 1981, the plane could carry 150 passengers at flew at 600mph over distances exceeding 4,000 miles. From 1965 they were also used as strategic air transports for the RAF.

CARS OF THE DECADE

The importance of personal transport increased dramatically during the Sixties and three of the images inextricably linked with the decade are the three-wheeler 'bubble car', the sleek, sexy, elongated E-type Jaguar and VW Camper Van.

In The 1960s

Mods and Rockers
Scooters v Motor Bikes

Mods and Rockers were two rival British youth sub-cultures of the 1960's with a tendency to riot on Brighton beach.

They had very different outlooks: The Mods thought of themselves as sophisticated, stylish and in touch with the times. The motor cycling centred Rockers thought the Mods effeminate snobs!

They had very different appearances: Mods centred on fashion and wore suits or other clean-cut outfits. The Rockers wore black leather jackets and motorcycle boots or sometimes, 'brothel creeper' shoes.

They had very different tastes in music. The Mods favoured Soul and African American R&B. The Rockers went for Rock 'n Roll.

So not surprisingly, they had very different tastes in transport.

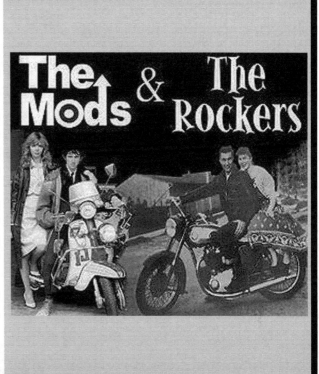

The Hovercraft

The great British invention of the decade was the Hovercraft. It was developed by Briton, Sir Christopher Cockerell. Saunders Roe, the flying boat firm at Cowes on the Isle of Wight built the prototype SR.N1, 20ft craft which first took to the seas in July 1959, crossing the English Channel from Calais to Dover in two hours with the inventor onboard. In 1961 hovercraft skirts were introduced to the design which provided far greater performance abilities and sea keeping.

The Hovercraft was a revolution in sea travel and the 1960's saw a fleet of craft crossing from the south coast to the Isle of Wight. They are now used throughout the world as specialised transports in disaster relief, coastguard, military and survey applications, as well as for sport or passenger service.

1970 - 1974

1970:

Jan: The age of majority for most legal purposes was reduced from 21 to 18 under terms of the Family Law Reform Act 1969.

Mar: Ian Smith declares Rhodesia a Republic and the British government refuses to recognise the new state.

1971:

Feb: Decimal Day. The UK and the Republic of Ireland both change to decimal currency.

Mar: The 'Daily Sketch', Britain's oldest tabloid newspaper is absorbed by the 'Daily Mail' after 62 years.

1972:

June: The 'Watergate' scandal begins in Richard Nixon's administration in the US.

Sep: The school leaving age in the UK was raised from 15 to 16 for pupils leaving at the end of the academic year.

1973:

Jan: The United Kingdom joins the European Economic Community, later to become the EU.

Sep: The IRA detonate bombs in Manchester and Victoria Station London and two days later, Oxford St. and Sloane Square.

1974:

Jan: Until March, the 3-day week is introduced by the Conservative Government to conserve electricity during the miners' strike.

Nov: 21 people are killed and 182 injured when the IRA set bombs in two Birmingham pubs.

1974: McDonald's open their first UK restaurant in South London. The traditional café was losing out, slow ordering and service with food served at tables was not as appealing as the clean, fast service and lower prices of this new fast food.

1974: In February, Harold Wilson becomes Prime Minister for the second time (first 1964-70) with a minority Government after Edward Heath resigns having failed to clinch a coalition with the Liberals. In the second general election of the year in October, Labour win with a majority of only 3 seats.

In June and July 1976, the UK experienced a heat wave. Temperatures peak at 35.9° and the whole country suffers a severe drought. Forest fires broke out, crops failed, and reservoirs dried up causing serious water shortages. The heatwave also produced swarms of ladybirds across the south and east.

On the 7th June, 1977, more than one million people lined the streets of London to watch the Queen and Prince Phillip lead a procession in the golden state coach, to St Paul's at the start of a week of the Queen's Silver Jubilee celebrations – 25 years on the throne. People all over the country held street or village parties to celebrate, more than 100,000 cards were received by the Queen and 30,000 Jubilee medals were given out.

1975 - 1979

1975:
Feb: Margaret Thatcher defeats Edward Heath to become the first female leader of the Conservative Party.

Apr: The Vietnam War ends with the Fall of Saigon to the Communists. South Vietnam surrenders unconditionally.

1976:
Mar: Harold Wilson announces his resignation as Prime Minister and James Callaghan is elected to the position in April.

Oct: The Intercity 125 high speed passenger train is introduced. Initially Paddington to Bristol and south Wales.

1977:
Jan: Jimmy Carter is sworn in as the 39th President of the United States, succeeding Gerald Ford.

Sep: Freddie Laker launches his 'Skytrain' with a single fare, Gatwick to New York, at £59 compared to £189.

1978:
Aug: Louise Brown becomes the world's first human born 'in vitro fertilisation' – test tube baby.

Nov: An industrial dispute shuts down The Times newspaper – until November 1979.

1979:
Mar: Airey Neave, politician and WW2 veteran, is blown up in the House of Commons carpark by the Irish National Liberation Army.

May: Margaret Thatcher becomes the first female Prime Minister of the United Kingdom. The Conservatives win a 43 seat majority.

Increasing Comfort and Prosperity

Homes became brighter and more comfortable in the 1970's. Teenagers could lie on the 'impossible to clean', loopy shag pile carpet watching films on VHS video cassettes or watch live programmes on the family's colour television set.

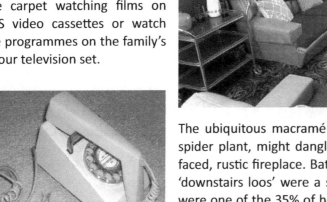

A Trimphone

The ubiquitous macramé owl, or plant holder complete with trailing spider plant, might dangle in the corner adjacent to the bulky, stone faced, rustic fireplace. Bathroom suites were often Avocado green and 'downstairs loos' were a statement of the houseowners ideals! If you were one of the 35% of households in Britain to own a telephone, you could catch up with friends and family on the new 'warbling' Trimphone, maybe sitting on your bright, floral covered couch.

Labour Saving Devices

The previous decade had been prosperous and the advances in technology continued such that by the 1970s, most households had many labour-saving devices. Sales of freezers rose rapidly in the 70s and by 1974, one in ten households had a freezer - mainly full of peas, chips and fish fingers but also ice cream, previously a rare treat, and in large quantities. Bulk buying food meant less time shopping and the Magimix food processor which added a choice of blades and attachments to a standard liquidiser, made home cooking more adventurous.

IN THE 1970s

Teenage Home Entertainment

Teenagers covered their bedroom walls with posters of their favourite bands and actors, ranging from Rod Stewart and the Boomtown Rats to Olivia Newton-John and Robert Redford. The lucky ones listening to top ten singles on their own stereo record deck which had replaced the old Dansette player.

If they wanted to play the new video games, they typically went to an arcade, but in 1975, Atari PONG was released, the first commercially successful video game you could play at home on your television. Based on a simple two-dimensional graphical representation of a tennis-like game, two players used paddles to hit a ball back and forth on a black and white screen. It captivated audiences and its success influenced developers to invent more and increasingly sophisticated games for the home market.

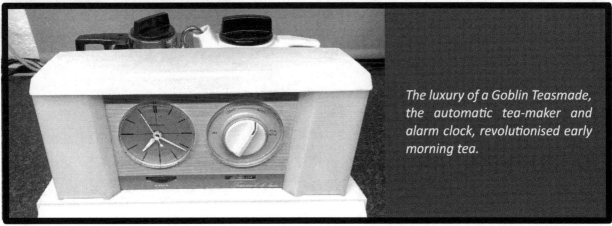

The luxury of a Goblin Teasmade, the automatic tea-maker and alarm clock, revolutionised early morning tea.

1970 - 1974

1970 Laurence Olivier becomes the first actor to be made a Lord. He is given a life peerage in the Queen's Birthday Honours list.
The first Glastonbury Festival was held, called the Worthy Farm Pop Festival. About 1500 attended.

1971 Coco Chanel, the French fashion designer died. (Born 1883)
The 'Blue Peter' presenters buried a time capsule in the grounds of BBC Television Centre, due to be opened on the first episode in 2000.
Mr Tickle, the first of the Mr Men books is published.

1972 'Jesus Christ Superstar', the Tim Rice & Andrew Lloyd Webber musical opens in the West End.
John Betjeman is appointed Poet Laureate.

1973 The British Library is established by merger of the British Museum Library & the National Lending Library for Science & Technology.
Series 1 of the BBC sitcom, 'Last of the Summer Wine' begins. There are eventually, 31 series.

1974 'Tinker, Tailor, Soldier, Spy' the first of John Le Carré's novel featuring the ageing spymaster, George Smiley, is published.
The Terracotta Army of Qin Shi Huang, thousands of life-size clay models of soldiers, horses and chariots, is discovered at Xi'an in China.

Milton Keynes Shopping Centre

1975 - 1979

1975 Donald Coggan is enthroned as the Archbishop of Canterbury.
Bill Gates and Paul Allen found Microsoft in Albuquerque, New Mexico.

1976 Trevor Nunn's memorable production of 'Macbeth' opens at Stratford-upon-Avon, with Ian McKellan and Judi Dench in the lead roles.
The Royal National Theatre on the South Bank opens.
Agatha Christie's last novel, Sleeping Murder, a Miss Marple story is published posthumously.

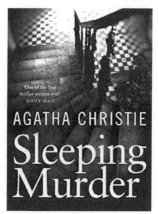

1977 Luciano Pavarotti makes his television debut singing in Puccini's La Boheme in the television debut of 'Live from the Met'.
Mike Leigh's satire on the aspirations and tastes of the new middle class emerging in the 70's, 'Abigail's Party', opened at the Hampstead Theatre starring Alison Steadman.

1978 The Andrew Lloyd Webber musical 'Evita' opens in London.
The arcade video game, 'Space Invaders' is released.

1979 Margaret Thatcher opens the new Central Milton Keynes Shopping Centre, the largest indoor shopping centre in Britain.
Anthony Blunt, British art historian and former Surveyor of the Queen's Pictures, in exposed as a double agent for the Soviets during WW2.
The Sony Walkman, portable cassette player is released.

IN THE 1970s

Pavarotti at the Met.

It was in his third season at the Metropolitan Opera House in New York that Luciano Pavarotti, the operatic tenor, would skyrocket to stardom. The company imported Covent Garden's production of Donizetti's *La Fille du Régiment* in 1972 as a vehicle for Joan Sutherland. The great Australian diva enjoyed a huge triumph, but the surprise for the audience was the young Italian tenor by her side who shared an equal part in the phenomenal success. This was the historic first Met performance telecast live on PBS as part of the long-running series that continues to the present day.

The Terracotta Army

'The Qin Tomb Terracotta Warriors and Horses' was constructed between 246-206BC as an afterlife guard for China's First Emperor, Qin Shihuang, from whom, China gets its name. He ordered it built to remember the army he led to triumph over other warring states, and to unite China.

The tomb and the army were all made by hand by some 700,000 artisans and labourers, and comprises thousands of life-size soldiers, each with different facial features and expressions, clothing, hairstyles and gestures, arranged in battle array.

All figures face east, towards the ancient enemies of Qin State, in rectangular formations and three separate vaults include rows of kneeling and standing archers, chariot war configurations and mixed forces of infantry, horse drawn chariots plus numerous soldiers armed with long spears, daggers and halberds.

FILMS

1970 - 1974

1970 Love Story, was the biggest grossing film a sentimental, tearjerker with the oft-quoted tagline, "Love means never having to say you're sorry." Nominated for the Academy Awards Best Picture, it was beaten by **Patton** which won 7 major titles that year.

1971 The Oscar winner was **The French Connection** with Gene Hackman as a New York police detective, Jimmy 'Popeye' Doyle, chasing down drug smugglers. Hackman was at the peak of his career in the 70's.

1972 Francis Ford Coppola's gangster saga, **The Godfather** became the highest grossing film of its time and helped drive a resurgence in the American film industry.

1973 Glenda Jackson won Best Actress for her role in **A Touch of Class.** She revealed that she was approached for the part by the director after appearing in the 1971 'Antony & Cleopatra' sketch on the Morecambe & Wise show. After she won, Eric Morecambe sent her a telegram saying, "Stick with us and we will get you another one".

1974 New films this year included **The Godfather Part II,** which won the Oscar, **Blazing Saddles** the comedy western and the disaster film, **The Towering Inferno** starring Paul Newman and Steve McQueen.

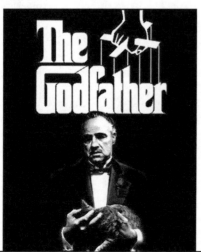

1975 - 1979

1975 One Flew Over the Cuckoo's Nest, an allegorical film set in a mental hospital, starring Jack Nicholson, beat tough competition for Best Picture from Spielberg's **Jaws** and Altman's **Nashville.**

1976 Jodi Foster won an Oscar in Martin Scorsese's gritty film **Taxi Driver** which examines alienation in urban society but it was Sylvester Stallone's **Rocky** that carried off the Best Picture award.

1977 Annie Hall from Woody Allen, the winner of Best Picture is a masterpiece of witty and quotable one-liners.

1978 The Vietnam War is examined through the lives of three friends from a small steel-mill town before, during and after their service in **The Deer Hunter**. A powerful and disturbing film.

1979 In this year's Best Picture, **Kramer v Kramer** there is a restaurant scene where Dustin Hoffman throws his wine glass at the wall. Only the cameraman was forewarned, Meryl Streep's shocked reaction was genuine!

Star Wars

Star Wars all began with George Lucas's eponymous film in 1977. The epic space fantasy, telling the adventures of characters "A long time ago in a galaxy far, far away", and this first film was a world beater in special effects technology using new computerised and digital effects. It rapidly became a phenomenon, Luke Skywalker, Jedi Knights, Princess Leia and Darth Vader becoming household names. An immensely valuable franchise grew up to include the films, television series, video games, books, comics and theme parks which now amounts to billions of dollars and the film introduced the phrase "May the Force be with you" into common usage.

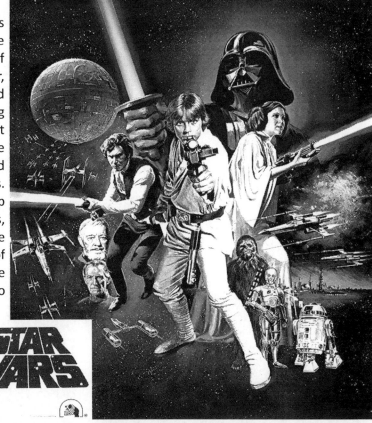

TWENTIETH CENTURY-FOX Presents A LUCASFILM LTD PRODUCTION STAR WARS
Starring MARK HAMILL HARRISON FORD CARRIE FISHER
PETER CUSHING
and
ALEC GUINNESS
Written and Directed by   Produced by   Music by
GEORGE LUCAS GARY KURTZ JOHN WILLIAMS
PANAVISION® PRINTS BY DE LUXE® TECHNICOLOR®
DOLBY SYSTEM

Apocalypse Now

Joseph Conrad's book 'Heart of Darkness' was the inspiration for producer and director Francis Ford Coppola's psychological film, a metaphor for the madness and folly of war itself for a generation of young American men. Beautiful, with symbolic shots showing the confusion, violence and fear of the nightmare of the Vietnam War, much of it was filmed on location in the Philippines where expensive sets were destroyed by severe weather, a typhoon called 'Olga', Marlon Brando showed up on set overweight and completely unprepared and Martin Sheen had a near-fatal heart attack.

This led to the film being two and a half times over budget and taking twice the number of scheduled weeks to shoot. When filming finally finished, the release was postponed several times as Coppola had six hours of film to edit. The helicopter attack scene with the 'Ride of the Valkyries' soundtrack is one of the most memorable film scenes ever.

FASHION

Women Wear the Trousers

It is often said that 1970s styles had no direction and were too prolific. French couture no longer handed down diktats of what we should be wearing, and the emerging street style was inventive, comfortable, practical for women or glamorous. It could be home-made, it was whatever you wanted it to be, and the big new trend was for gender neutral clothes, women wore trousers in every walk of life, trouser suits for the office, jeans at home and colourful, tight-fitting ones for in between. Trouser legs became wider and 'bell-bottoms', flared from the knee down, with bottom leg openings of up to twenty-six inches, made from denim, bright cotton and satin polyester, became mainstream. Increasingly 'low cut', they were teamed with platform soles or high cut boots until they could not flare anymore, and so, by the end of the decade they had gone, skin-tight trousers, in earth tones, greys, whites and blacks were much more in vogue.

And the Hot Pants

In the early 70s, women's styles were very flamboyant with extremely bright colours and, in the winter, long, flowing skirts and trousers *but* come the summer, come the Hot Pants. These extremely short shorts were made of luxury fabrics such as velvet and satin designed for fashionable wear, not the practical equivalents for sports or leisure, and they enjoyed great popularity until falling out of fashion in the middle of the decade. Teamed with skin-tight t-shirts, they were favourites for clubwear and principally worn by women, including Jacqueline Kennedy Onassis, Elizabeth Taylor and Jane Fonda, but they were also worn by some high-profile men, David Bowie, Sammy Davis Jnr and Liberace among them, although the shorts were slightly longer than the women's versions, but still shorter than usual. Chest hair, medallions, sideburns and strangely, tennis headbands, finished the look!

In The 1970s

These Boots Are Made For Walking

Boots were so popular in the early 1970s that even men were getting in on the action. It wasn't uncommon to see a man sporting 2" inch platform boots inspired by John Travolta in Saturday Night Fever. The trend was all about being sexy on the dance floor!

And Punk Was Not to Be Ignored

Emerging in the mid 70s in London as an anarchic and aggressive movement, a few hundred young people defined themselves as an anti-fashion urban youth street culture closely aligned to the music that became punk. They cut up old clothes from charity shops, destroyed the fabric and refashioned outfits in a manner intended to shock. Trousers were deliberately torn to reveal laddered tights and dirty legs and worn with heavy Doc Martens footwear, now seen on many young women too.

Safety pins and chains held bits of fabric together. Neck chains were made from padlocks and chain and even razor blades were used as pendants. Body piercings and studs, beginning with the three-stud earlobe, progressing to the ear outline embedded with ear studs, evolved to pins in eyebrows, cheeks, noses or lips and together with tattoos were the beginning of unisex fashion. All employed by male and female alike to offend. Vivienne Westwood and Malcolm McLaren quickened the style with her bondage shop "Sex", and his punk music group, the "Sex Pistols".

Saturday Morning TV

In the early 70s, Saturday mornings for many children still meant a trip to the cinema but with the advent of Saturday Morning Television, under instruction 'not to wake their parents', children could creep downstairs, switch on the box and stay entertained until lunchtime.

First, in 1974, came ITV's 'Tiswas', hosted by Chris Tarrant it was a chaotic blend of jokes, custard pies and buckets of water.

Then in 1976, the BBC introduced 'Swap Shop' with Noel Edmonds, Keith Chegwin and John Craven and a Saturday morning ritual was born. Nearly three hours of ground-breaking television using the 'phone-in' extensively for the first time on TV. The programme included music, competitions, cartoons and spontaneous nonsense from Edmonds. There was coverage of news and issues relevant to children, presented by 'Newsround's' John Craven but by far the most popular element of the show was the "Swaporama" open-air event, hosted by Chegwin. An outside broadcast unit would travel to different locations throughout the UK where sometimes as many as 2000 children would gather to swap their belongings with others.

Saturday Night Fever

Memories of Saturday night and Sunday morning in the discotheque. A mirror ball; strobe lights; 'four on the floor' rhythm; the throb of the bass drum; girls in Spandex tops with hot pants or vividly coloured, shiny, Lycra trousers with equally dazzling halter neck tops; boys in imitations of John Travolta's white suit from Saturday Night Fever risking life and limb on towering platform shoes.

These glamorous dancers, clad in glitter, metallic lame and sequins, gyrating as the music pounded out at the direction of the DJ, whirling energetically and glowing bright 'blue-white' under the ultra-violet lights as their owners 'strutted their stuff', perspiration running in rivulets down their backs.

The DJs, stars in their own right, mixed tracks by Donna Summer, the Bee Gees, Gloria Gaynor, Sister Sledge, Chic and Chaka Khan, as their sexy followers, fuelled by the night club culture of alcohol and drugs, changed from dancing the Hustle with their partners to the solo freestyle dancing of John Travolta.

In The 1970s

The Dangers of Leisure

In the 1970's the Government was intent on keeping us all – and particularly children – safe and continued producing the wartime Public Information Films, which were still scaring children witless!

1971: Children and Disused Fridges: Graphic warnings of children being suffocated in old fridges that, tempted by their playful imaginations, they want to climb into.

1973: Broken Glass: This film shows a boy running on the sand, ending abruptly before he steps on a broken glass bottle, the film urges people to use a bin or take their litter home with them.

1974: The Fatal Floor: This 30 second film had the message, "Polish a floor, put a rug on it, and you might as well set a man trap..."

1979: Play Safe – Frisbee: This film used chilling electronic music and frightening sound effects to highlight the potentially fatal combination of frisbees with electricity pylons and kites, fishing rods and radio-controlled planes.

1972: Teenagers – Learn to Swim:

A cartoon aimed at teenagers warns them to learn how to swim, or risk social embarrassment and failure to attract the opposite sex. The female character's illusion of her boyfriend 'Dave' being able 'to do anything' is shattered after she wishes they were at the seaside, where she discovers Dave can't swim. He in turn wishes he didn't 'keep losing me birds' after his girlfriend disappears with 'Mike' who 'swims like a fish'. Although the film is light-hearted in tone it was intended in part to help prevent accidents.

1975: Protect and Survive:

This was the title of a series of booklets and films made in the late 1970s and early 1980s, dealing with emergency planning for a nuclear war including the recognition of attack warning, fallout warning, and all-clear signals, the preparation of a home "fallout room" and the stockpiling of food, water, and other emergency supplies. In the opinion of some contemporary critics, the films *were deeply and surprisingly fatalistic in tone*!

MUSIC

1970 - 1974

1970 Number 1 for 3 weeks, **Bridge Over Troubled Water** by Simon and Garfunkel became their 'signature song' selling over 6m copies worldwide. It also became one of the most performed songs of the 20th century, covered by over 50 artists.

1971 George Harrison's first release as a solo **My Sweet Lord** topped the charts for five weeks and became the best selling UK single of the year.
Rod Stewart had 7 No 1's this year including in October, the double sided hits, **Reason to Believe/Maggie May**

1972 A jingle, rewritten to become the hugely popular 'Buy the world a Coke' advert for the Coca Cola company, was re-recorded by The New Seekers as the full-length song, **I'd Like to Teach the World to Sing**, which stayed at No 1 for 4 weeks.

1973 Dawn featuring Tony Orlando had the bestselling single of 1973 with **"Tie a Yellow Ribbon Round the 'Ole Oak Tree"**, which spent four weeks at the top spot and lasted 11 weeks in the top ten.
Queen released their debut album, **"Queen"**. The Carpenters reached number 2 with **"Yesterday Once More"**.

1974 **Waterloo**, the winning song for Sweden in the Eurovision Song Contest began ABBA's journey to world-wide fame.
David Essex has his first No 1 with **Wanna Make You a Star** which spends 3 weeks at the top of the charts.

1975 - 1979

1975 **Make Me Smile** (Come Up and See Me) was a chart topper for Steve Harley & Cockney Rebel. **Bohemian Rhapsody** for Queen, stayed at the top for nine weeks.

1976 The Brotherhood of Man won the Eurovision Song Contest for Great Britain with **Save Your Kisses for Me**. It became the biggest-selling song of the year and remains one of the biggest-selling Eurovision winners ever.
Don't Go Breaking My Heart was the first No. 1 single in the UK for both Elton John and Kiki Dee.

1977 Actor David Soul, riding high on his success in Starsky & Hutch, had the No 1 spot for 4 weeks with **Don't Give Up on Us**.
Way Down was the last song to be recorded by Elvis Presley before his death and stayed at No 1 for 5 weeks.

1978 Kate Bush released her debut single, **Wuthering Heights,** which she had written aged 18 after watching Emily Brontë's Wuthering Heights on television and discovering she shared the author's birthday.
Spending five weeks at the top of the British charts, Boney M's **"Rivers of Babylon"** became the biggest selling single of the year, exceeding one million sales between May and June.

1979 Frequently recalled as a symbol of female empowerment, **I Will Surviv**e reached the top for Gloria Gaynor.
The Wall, Pink Floyd's rock opera was released, featuring all three parts of **Another Brick in the Wall. Part 2**, written as a protest against rigid schooling was No1 in Dec.

IN THE 1970s

The Decade in Numbers

Most No1 Singles:
ABBA with seven.
Waterloo (1974);
Mamma Mia, Fernando
and
Dancing Queen (all 1976);
**Knowing Me Knowing You,
The Name of the Game,**
(both 1977);
Take a Chance on Me
(1978).

Most Weeks at No 1:
Bohemian Rhapsody by
Queen; **Mull of Kintyre /
Girl's School** by Wings;
You're the One That I Want
by John Travolta and Olivia
Newton-John.

WINGS

MULL OF KINTYRE

'Danny' and 'Sandy' Fever

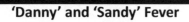

Grease, the 1978 musical romantic comedy starring John Travolta (Danny) and Olivia Newton-John (Sandy) had phenomenal success. In June to August 1978, **You're the One That I Want** and in September to October, **Summer Nights**, locked up the number 1 position for a total of sixteen weeks.

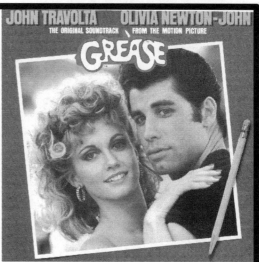

Hopelessly Devoted to You was nominated for an Oscar and John Travolta and Olivia Newton-John seemed to be constantly in the public conscience. Critically and commercially successful, the soundtrack album ended 1978 as the second best -selling album in the US, behind the soundtrack of the 1977 blockbuster **Saturday Night Fever,** which also starred John Travolta.

SCIENCE AND NATURE

Pocket Calculators

The first pocket calculators came onto the market towards the end of 1970. In the early 70s they were an expensive status symbol but by the middle of the decade, businessmen were quite used to working their sales figures out quickly whilst 'out of the office'.

Household accounts were made easy and children wished they could use them at school – not just to help with homework. Most early calculators performed only basic addition, subtraction, multiplication and division but the speed and accuracy, sometimes giving up to 12 digit answers, of the machine proved sensational.

In 1972, Hewlett Packard introduced the revolutionary HP-35 pocket calculator which, in addition to the basic operations, enabled advanced mathematical functions. It was the first scientific, hand-held calculator, able to perform a wide number of logarithmic and trigonometric functions, store intermediate solutions and utilise scientific notations.

With intense competition, prices of pocket calculators dropped rapidly, and the race was on to produce the smallest possible models. The target was to be no bigger than a credit card. Casio won the race.

The Miracle of IVF

In 1971, Patrick Steptoe, gynaecologist, Robert Edwards, biologist, and Jean Purdy, nurse and embryologist set up a small laboratory at the Kershaw's Hospice in Oldham which was to lead to the development of in vitro fertilisation and eventual birth of Louise Brown in 1978.

They developed a technique for retrieving eggs at the right time and fertilising them in the laboratory, believing that they could be implanted back in the uterus. It took more than 80 embryo transfers before the first successful pregnancy, and the birth of Louise, the first 'test-tube baby', heralded the potential happiness of infertile people and a bright future for British science and industry.

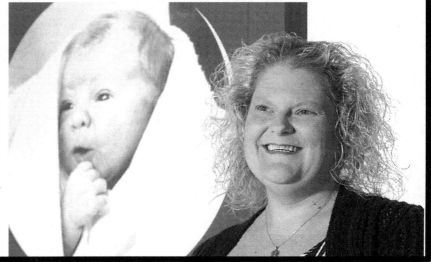

IN THE 1970s

"Houston We Have a Problem"

In April 1970, two days after the launch of Apollo 13, the seventh crewed mission in the Apollo space program and the third meant to land on the Moon, the NASA ground crew heard the now famous message, "Houston, we've had a problem." An oxygen tank had exploded, and the lunar landing was aborted leaving the astronauts in serious danger. The crew looped around the Moon and returned safely to Earth, their safe return being down to the ingenuity under pressure by the crew, commanded by Jim Lovell, together with the flight controllers and mission control. The crew experienced great hardship, caused by limited power, a chilly and wet cabin and a shortage of drinking water.

Even so, Apollo 13 set a spaceflight record for the furthest humans have travelled from Earth.

Tens of millions of viewers watched Apollo 13 splashdown in the South Pacific Ocean and the recovery by USS Iwo Jima.

The global campaigning network **Greenpeace** was founded in 1971 by Irving and Dorothy Stowe, environmental activists. The network now has 26 independent national or regional organisations in 55 countries worldwide.

Their stated goal is to ensure the ability of the earth to nurture life in all its diversity. To achieve this they "use non-violent, creative confrontation to expose global environmental problems, and develop solutions for a green and peaceful future". In detail to:

- Stop the planet from warming beyond 1.5° in order to prevent the most catastrophic impacts of the climate breakdown.
- Protect biodiversity in all its forms.
- Slow the volume of hyper-consumption and learn to live within our means.
- Promote renewable energy as a solution that can power the world.
- Nurture peace, global disarmament and non-violence.

1970 - 1974

1970 The thoroughbred 'Nijinsky', wins all three English Triple Crown Races: **The 2,000 Guineas** at Newmarket; **The Derby** at Epsom; the **St. Leger Stakes** at Doncaster and the Irish Derby. The first horse to do this in 35 years and not repeated as of 2021.

1971 Arsenal wins both the **First Division** title and the **FA Cup**, becoming the fourth team ever to win the double.
Jack Nicklaus wins his ninth major at the **PGA Championship**, the first golfer ever to win all four majors for the second time.

1972 At **Wimbledon**, Stan Smith (US) beat Ilie Nastase in the Men's Singles Final. It was his only Wimbledon title.
In the Women's Final, Billie Jean King (US) beat Yvonne Goolagong (AUS) to gain her fourth **Wimbledon** title.
The **Olympic Games** held in Munich are overshadowed by the murder of eleven Israeli athletes and coaches by Palestinian Black September members.

1973 George Foreman knocks out Joe Frazier in only two rounds to take the **World Heavyweight Boxing** Championship title.

Red Rum wins the **Grand National** with a new record and staging a spectacular comeback on the run-in having trailed the leader by 15 lengths at the final fence.

1974 Liverpool win the **FA Cup Final** against Newcastle United at Wembley. Kevin Keegan scored two of their three goals.
Eddie Merckx wins the **Tour de France**, becoming the first rider to win the Triple Crown of Cycling, **Tour de France**, **Giro d'Italia** and **World Championships** in one calendar year.

1975 - 1979

1975 In athletics, John Walker (NZ) sets a new world record becoming the first man to **run a mile** in under 3 mins 50 seconds. He clocks 3mins 49.4 secs.
Muhammad Ali defeats Joe Frazier in the 'Thrilla In Manilla' to maintain the **Boxing Heavyweight Championship** of the world.

1976 The **Olympics** are held in Montreal. Britain's only medal is a Bronze, won by Brendan Foster running the **10,000 metres**.
John Curry, becomes the **European, Olympic and World Figure Skating Champion**. He was the first skater to combine, ballet and modern dance into his skating.

1977 The commercial **World Series Cricket** was introduced by Kerry Packer. WSC changed the nature of the game with its emphasis on the "gladiatorial" aspect of fast bowling and heavy promotion of fast bowlers.

1978 During the **Oxford and Cambridge Boat Race,** the Cambridge boat sinks. It is the first sinking in the race since 1951.
Wales wins the rugby **Five Nations Championship** and completes the Grand Slam having beaten England, France, Ireland and Scotland.

1978 Arsenal beat Manchester United 3-2 in the **FA Cup Final.**
At **The Open** at Royal Lytham & St Annes Golf Club Seve Ballesteros becomes the first golfer from Continental Europe to win a major since 1907.

In The 1970s

Traffic Lights and Football

Before the introduction of Red and Yellow Cards in football, cautions or sending a player off had to be dealt with orally, and the language barrier could sometimes present problems. For example, in the 1966 World Cup, the German referee tried in vain to send Argentinian player Antonio Rattin off the field, but Rattin did not 'want' to understand and eventually was escorted off the pitch by the police!

Ken Aston, Head of World Cup Referees, was tasked with solving this problem and legend has it that the idea of the red and yellow cards came to him when he was stopped in his car at traffic lights. They were tested in the 1968 Olympics and the 1970 World Cup in Mexico and introduced to European leagues soon after and after six years, to English football.

In 1976, the first player to be sent off using a red card in an English game was Blackburn Rovers winger David Wagstaffe.

Tour de France

In 1974 the Tour de France covered 2,546 miles in 22 stages, one of which was the first to be held in the UK, a circuit stage on the Plympton By-pass near Plymouth. Eddy Merckx of Belgium won eight stages and won the race overall with a comfortable margin, making it five wins for him out of his five Tours. He also won that year's Combination Classification – the General (Yellow Jersey), Points or Sprint (Green Jersey) and Mountains (since 1975, King of the Mountains wears the Polka Dot Jersey).

Rockstar and Racing Driver

James Hunt, the charismatic, play-boy darling of the press in the 1970's, began his Formula 1 career at the beginning of the decade with the Hesketh Racing team and gave them their only win in 1975 at the Dutch GP. He moved to McLaren in 1976, and in his first year with them, he and his great rival Niki Lauda at Ferrari, fought an epic season-long battle. It was an extraordinarily dramatic season, over sixteen races filled with drama and controversy, where Lauda had gained an early championship lead. By the final race in Japan, he was being reeled-in by Hunt and was only three points ahead. Hunt drove the race of his life, in the worst possible weather conditions, to finish in third place. Lauda, already badly injured from the crash at Nürburgring in August, withdrew because of the hazardous conditions which meant James Hunt became World Champion, winning by just a single point.

Hunt's natural driving ability was phenomenal, and while his habit of risk-taking didn't always endear him to others, hence the nickname "Hunt the Shunt", it also made him compelling to watch. Off track, he and Niki had an enduring friendship, which lasted after James's retirement from F1 in 1979 until his untimely death from a heart attack in 1993, aged just 45.

TRANSPORT

ICONIC MACHINES OF THE DECADE

The Jumbo Jet
Entered service on January 22, 1970. The 747 was the first airplane dubbed a "Jumbo Jet", the first wide-body airliner.

In 1971 Ford launched the car that was to represent the 1970s, the Cortina Mk III. In 1976 the Mk IV and 1979 Mk V. Cortinas were the best-selling cars of the decade.

The best-selling foreign import was the Datsun Sunny, which was only the 19th best-selling car of the decade.

In 1973, British Leyland's round, dumpy shaped Allegro was not at all popular and meagre sales contributed greatly to BL's collapse in 1975.

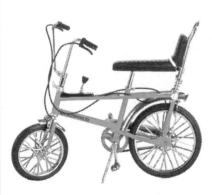

Raleigh Chopper
Shot to fame in the 70's when every child, and some adults, wanted one. It had a high back, long seat and motorbike rear wheel and was probably the first bike to have a centrally positioned gear shift.

IN THE 1970s

Women Drivers

In 1974, Jill Viner became the first female bus driver for London Transport. She trained to become a bus driver at a centre in Chiswick in 1974, when London Transport were said to be 3,200 drivers short

While women had previously driven buses within bus depots during the Second World War, Viner was the first women to drive a bus in service in London. In the weeks after she started driving, it was reported that thirty women had applied to become bus drivers.

In 1978, Hannah Dadds completed a seven-week training course to qualify as a train driver and became the first female driver on the London Underground.

Hannah's sister Edna also joined the London Underground working first as a guard and then a driver. Hannah and Edna became the first all-female crew on the London Underground.

Concorde

The Anglo-French supersonic passenger airliner had a take-off speed of 220 knots (250mph) and a cruising speed of 1350mph – more than twice the speed of sound. With seating for 92 to 128 passengers, Concorde entered service in 1976 and operated for 27 years.

Twenty aircraft were built in total, including six prototypes and in the end, only Air France and British Airways purchased and flew them, due in great part to supersonic flights being restricted to ocean-crossing routes, to prevent sonic boom disturbance over land and populated areas. Concorde flew regular transatlantic flights from London and Paris to New York, Washington, Dulles in Virginia and Barbados and the BA Concorde made just under 50,000 flights and flew more than 2.5m passengers supersonically.

A typical London to New York crossing would take a little less than three and a half hours as opposed to about eight hours for a subsonic flight.

The aircraft was retired in 2003, three years after the crash of an Air France flight in which all passengers and crew were killed.

THE MAJOR NEWS STORIES

1980 - 1984

1980:

May: Mount St. Helens experiences a huge eruption that creates avalanches, explosions, large ash clouds, mudslides, and massive damage. 57 people are killed.

Dec: John Lennon, the former Beatle, age 40, is shot and killed by an obsessed fan in Manhattan.

1981:

July: Prince Charles marries Lady Diana Spencer at St Paul's Cathedral.

Margaret Thatcher's Government begins the privatisation of the Nationalised Industries.

1982:

Apr: Argentina invades the Falkland Islands and the UK retakes possession of them by the end of June.

May: Pope John Paul II visits the United Kingdom. It is the first visit by a reigning Pope

1983:

Apr: The £1 coin is introduced in the UK.

Jun: Margaret Thatcher wins a landslide victory for the Conservatives in the General Election, with a majority of 144.

Nov: The first United States cruise missiles arrive at RAF Greenham Common in Berkshire

1984:

Mar: The National Mineworkers Union led by Arthur Scargill, begin what will be a year-long strike against the National Coal Board's plans to shut 20 collieries

May: The Thames Barrier, designed to protect London from floods, is opened by9The Queen

1980: Mount St. Helens before and after the eruption. The top third of the mountain was blown away.

1982: EPCOT opened at Disney World in Florida, "...an experimental prototype community of tomorrow that will take its cue from the new ideas and technologies that are now emerging ... a showcase of the ingenuity and imagination of American free enterprise." - *Walt Disney*

1984: On 31 October, Indira Gandhi, Prime Minister of India, was killed by her Sikh bodyguards.
The assassination sparked four days of riots that left more than 8,000 Indian Sikhs dead in revenge attacks.

1985 - 1989

1985: On 1st January, Ernie Wise made the first, civilian, mobile phone call in the UK from outside the Dicken's Inn at St Katharine's Dock. Via the Vodafone network he called their office in Newbury on a VT1 which weighed 5.5kg.

1987: Oct 15th: Weather-man Michael Fish: "Earlier on today, a woman rang the BBC and said she heard there was a hurricane on the way... well, if you're watching, don't worry, there isn't!". That night, hurricane force winds hit much of the South of England killing 23 people, bringing down an estimated 15 million trees and causing damage estimated at £7.3 billion.

1985:

Jan: The Internet's Domain Name System is created and the country code top-level domain .uk is registered in July.

Dec: The original charity "Comic Relief" is launched by Richard Curtis and Lenny Henry on Christmas Day,.

1986:

Apr: A Soviet Nuclear reactor at Chernobyl explodes causing the release of radioactive material across much of Europe.

Oct: The 'Big Bang' – the London Stock Exchange is deregulated allowing computerised share dealing.

1987:

Jan: Terry Waite, the special envoy of the Archbishop of Canterbury in Lebanon, is kidnapped in Beirut. He is held in captivity for 1,763 days until 1991.

Oct: Black Monday: Wall Street crash leads to £50,000,000,000 being wiped of the value of shares on the London stock exchange.

1988:

Dec: Suspected Libyan terrorist bomb explodes on Pan Am jet over Lockerbie in Scotland on December 21st killing all 259 on board and 11 on the ground.

Dec: Health Minister Edwina Currie states that most of Britain's egg production is infected with salmonella, causing an immediate nationwide slump in egg sales.

1989:

Apr: 94 fans are killed in the Hillsborough football stadium collapse in Sheffield. 3 more will die and over 300 are hospitalised.

Nov: The Fall of the Berlin Wall heralds the end of the Cold War and communism in East and Central Europe.

THE HOME

A Busier Life

In the 1980's, life became more stressful, there were two recessions, divorce rates were increasing, women were exercising their rights and these years were the beginning of the end of the traditional family unit. With single parent families or both parents at work and a generally 'busier' life, there was a fundamental change to the family and home. There was also a lot more choice.

Many more 'lower cost' restaurants, chilled ready-made meals, instant foods such as Findus Crispy Pancakes, Pot Noodles or M&S Chicken Kievs and the, by now, ubiquitous tea bag, together with the consumer boom in electrical labour-saving devices from food processors and microwaves to dishwashers and automatic washing machines, sandwich toasters and jug kettles, all added up to more free time from housework and cooking.

Floral Décor

Flower patterns were all the rage in early 1980s home décor, with flower patterned upholstery and curtains to floral wallpapers taking over from the 70s woodchip paper.

Artex was still hugely popular on ceilings and walls, finished with the familiar stippled or swirled patterns and peach was *the* fashionable colour of choice for interior design schemes. Chintz curtains could have more layers, swags and tails than an onion! The bold reached the height of fashion with a red and black colour scheme, black ash furniture and a framed Ferrari print on the wall – with a bold wallpaper border at the ceiling which often clashed with the paper on the walls.

IN THE 1980s

The Telephone Answering Machine

There once was a time when, to use a telephone, both people had to be on the phone at the same time. You had to pick up the phone when it rang. The answering machine, one cassette tape for the outgoing message and one to record incoming calls, changed all that. By allowing people to take calls when they were away and respond to any message at a later time.

Children's Playtime

For children, toys of the early 80s had a bit of a 70s feel, Star Wars action figures, remote controlled cars and trucks, Barbie dolls and Action Men, but by 1983 there was a huge increase in toys like Transformers, Care Bears, a plethora of talking robot toys, My Little Pony, Teenage Mutant Ninja Turtles and Cabbage Patch Kids which was THE craze of 1983 – these odd looking 'little people' were the first images to feature on disposable 'designer' nappies!

Basic Atari video games evolved to Nintendo's NES game system and all of them competed with Apple and Sinclair home computers and personal Walkman stereos.

ART AND CULTURE

1980 - 1984

1980 "Who shot J.R.?" was an advertising catchphrase that CBS created to promote their TV show, 'Dallas', referring to the cliff hanger of the finale of the previous season. The episode, 'Who Done It?' aired in November with an estimated 83 million viewers tuning in.

MV Mi Amigo, the ship 'Radio Caroline', the pirate radio station, operates from, runs aground and sinks off Sheerness.

1981 A bronze statue of Charlie Chaplin, as his best loved character, The Tramp, is unveiled in Leicester Square.

1982 The D'Oyly Carte Opera Company gives its last performance at the end of a final London season, having been in near-continuous existence since 1875.

1983 Children's ITV is launched in Britain as a new branding for the late afternoon programming block on the ITV network.

1984 The comedian Tommy Cooper collapses and dies on stage from a heart attack during a live televised show, 'Live from Her Majesty's'.

Ted Hughes is appointed Poet Laureate and succeeds Sir John Betjeman. Philip Larkin had turned down the post.

1985 - 1989

1985 The Roux Brothers' Waterside Inn at Bray, Berkshire becomes the first establishment in the UK to be awarded three Michelin stars.

'Live Aid' pop concerts in London and Philadelphia raise over £50,000,000 for famine relief in Ethiopia.

1986 The Sun newspaper alleges that comedian Freddie Starr ate a live hamster.

More than 30m viewers watched the Christmas Day episode of 'East Enders' in which Den Watts serves the divorce papers on his wife Angie.

1987 Christie's auction house in London sells one of Vincent van Gogh's iconic Sunflowers paintings for £24,750,000 after a bidding war between two unidentified competitors bidding via telephone.

'The Simpsons' cartoon first appears as a series of animated short films on the 'Tracey Ullman Show' in the US.

1988 Salman Rushdie published 'The Satanic Verses' a work of fiction which caused a widespread furore and forced Rushdie to live in hiding out of fear for his life.

1989 Sky Television begins broadcasting as the first satellite TV service in Britain.

Remains of both The Rose, an Elizabethan playhouse, and the Globe Theatre are found in London.

The Great Musical Revival

By the start of the 1980's, Britain was in recession and the West End Theatres were facing rising costs and falling audiences – until the revival of the Musical, led by Andrew Lloyd Webber.

In 1981, his first 'unlikely' musical **Cats** led by Elaine Paige, went on to be the first 'megamusical' spectacular in the West End and on Broadway.

It was followed in 1984 by **Starlight Express.**

By now, these shows were being enjoyed not only by home audiences but also, a massive 44% of tickets, were purchased by tourists.

In 1986, the **Phantom of the Opera** opened to overwhelmingly positive reviews.

In 1987 **Les Misérables** brought the Royal Shakespeare Company 's expertise in high drama to the musical which was set amidst the French Revolution and brought fame to its writers, Alain Boubill and Claude-Michel Schönberg fame and producer Cameron Mackintosh his millions.

Other hit musicals of the decade: Willy Russel's **Blood Brothers**, Noël Gay's revival of **Me and My Girl**, and Lloyd Webber's **Aspects of Love.**

FILMS

1980 - 1984

1980 The epic **The Empire Strikes Back** is released and is the highest-grossing film of the year, just as its predecessor, **Star Wars** was in 1977. However, the Oscar for Best Picture went to **Ordinary People**, the psychological drama depicting the disintegration of an upper middle-class family in Illinois.

1981 Chariots of Fire based on the true story of two British athletes, one Christian, one Jewish in the 1924 Olympics, won the Academy Awards.
The film's title was inspired by the line "Bring me my Chariot of fire!" from Blake's poem adapted as the hymn 'Jerusalem'.

1982 Spielberg's science fiction film of **ET the Extra Terrestrial** was a huge box office hit this year, the scene when the little green extra-terrestrial learns to speak, instilled "ET phone home" into the collective memory. The rather more down to earth biographical film of Mahatma Gandhi **Gandhi**, picked up the Best Film award.

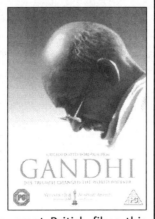

1983 There were many great British films this year including **Local Hero** and **Educating Rita, The Dresser** and Sean Connery playing Bond for the last time in **Never Say Never Again.** It was the American, **Terms of Endearment** that won the Oscars.

1984 Amadeus the fictionalised story of the composer Wolfgang Amadeus Mozart and a supposed rivalry with Italian composer Antonio Salieri, featuring much of Mozart's music, won the imagination of the audiences and the Best Film of the Year award too.

1985 - 1989

1985 Spielberg's 'coming of age' epic starring Whoopi Goldberg in her breakthrough role, **The Color Purple**, was nominated for eleven Academy Awards but failed to achieve a single win. The prize went to Meryl Streep and Robert Redford in the romantic drama, **Out of Africa.**

1986 The first of Oliver Stone's trilogy based on his experiences in the Vietnam war, **Platoon** picks up this year's Oscar for Best Film, beating two British nominations, **A Room with a View** and **The Mission.** This was also the year of the Australian box office runaway success, **Crocodile Dundee.**

1987 The thriller **Fatal Attraction** attracted both favourable reviews and controversy. It put the phrase 'bunny boiler' into the urban dictionary.

1988 Glenn Close was nominated for Best Actress for her role as the Marquise de Merteuil who plots revenge against her ex-lover, in **Dangerous Liaisons.** Dustin Hoffman and Tom Cruise starred in **Rainman**, the winner of Best Film of the year.

1989 Unusually, it was a PG rated film, **Driving Miss Daisy** that won the Academy Award this year, a gentle, heartwarming comedy which had the serious themes of racism and anti-semitism at its heart. Jessica Tandy at age 81, won Best Actress, the oldest winner to do so.

David Puttnam, Baron Puttnam of Queensgate (1997)

The 1980s saw the release of several films by the British producer, David Puttnam, beginning with, in 1981, his most successful film up until that time, **Chariots of Fire**.

His next big success was **Local Hero** the comedy drama, set on the west coast of Scotland where an American oil company wishes to purchase a local village and surrounding area.

Next, in 1984, came the acclaimed **Cal**, a young man on the fringes of the IRA who falls in love with a Catholic woman whose husband, a Protestant policeman, had been killed by the IRA one year earlier. Entered into the Cannes Film Festival, Helen Mirren won Best Actress.

Also in 1984, Puttnam produced **The Killing Fields**, a harrowing biographical drama about the Khmer Rouge in Cambodia, based on the experiences of a Cambodian journalist and an American journalist. This film received seven Oscar nominations and won three, most notably Best Supporting Actor for Haing S. Ngor who had no previous acting experience.

Puttnam's career spanned the 1960s to the 1990s and his films have won 10 Oscars, 31 BAFTAs, 13 Golden Globes, nine Emmys, four David di Donatellos in Italy and the Palme d'Or at Cannes.

FASHION

A Fashion Statement

The mid to late 80s was the time to 'make a statement'. The mass media took over fashion trends completely and fashion magazines, TV shows and music videos all played a part in dictating the latest bold fashions.

There was a huge emphasis on bright colours, huge shoulder pads, power suits which gave an exaggerated silhouette like an upside-down triangle, flashy skirts and spandex leggings, velour, leg warmers and voluminous parachute pants.

We wore iconic oversized plastic hoop earrings, rubber bracelets and shiny chain necklaces and huge sunglasses giving faces the appearance of large flies. Men and women alike made their hair 'big' with or without the ubiquitous teased perm and for the girls, glossy pink lips, overly filled-in brows, rainbow-coloured eyeshadows and exaggerated blusher were on trend.

Men too joined in with style and sported oversized blazers with shiny buttons, pinstripe two-piece suits and sweaters, preferably from Ralph Lauren, draped over the shoulders.

Polka Dots

Although not new to the 80s - Disney's Minnie Mouse was first seen in the 1920's wearing the red and white dottie print - polka dots were also very popular.

Bands such as The Beat used them in their music videos and well-known celebrities including Madonna and Princess Diana loved the cool look of polka dot dresses and tops.

When teamed with the oversized earrings of the decade and big hair, whilst bucking the trend for bright, gaudy colours, they still "made a statement".

Carolina Herrera used polka dots on most of her dresses during the late 1980s and early 1990s and it remains a key print in her collections, a classic.

As Marc Jacobs, the American designer famously said, "There is never a wrong time for a polka dot."

In The 1980s

Labels, logos and idols

Pale blue, distressed jeans were the fashionable 'street wear', worn semi fitted and held with a statement belt at the natural waistline. When the boy band Bros came along in 1988, wearing jeans ripped at the knee coupled with leather, slip on loafers, teens up and down the country enthusiastically took the scissors to their own jeans, and ripped, frayed or shredded them.
.

Pop Fashion
If you were into pop music in the 1980s, there's no doubt that superstar Madonna influenced what you wore.

Feet also presented a branding opportunity, Patrick Cox had celebrities make his loafers universally desired, and, often credited with kicking off the whole fashion sneaker movement, Nike Air 'Jordans' – named after basketball star, Michael Jordan – were launched in 1985. If you couldn't have them, then high-top Reebok sneakers were also the pinnacle of style -- as were Adidas Superstar kicks and matching tracksuits.

The Fitness Craze

The 1980's had a fitness craze. Celebrities made aerobics videos and endorsed weight loss products and equipment. Health Clubs and Gyms became the place to be and to be seen but were predominantly for men so for women who wanted to exercise in the privacy of their own home, by the mid '80s, there were very few households that didn't own at least one well-worn VHS copy of **'Jane Fonda's Workout'**.

Her 1982 video sold more than 17 million copies, with the actress wearing a striped and belted leotard, violet leggings and leg warmers, big, big hair and in full make-up and working up a sweat to some heavy synth music, inspired a whole generation.

At home, between 1983 and 1987, Britain's answer to Jane Fonda, Diana Moran **'The Green Goddess',** appeared on TV screens wearing her trade-mark green leotard telling millions of BBC Breakfast viewers to 'wake up and shape up' with her aerobics routines.

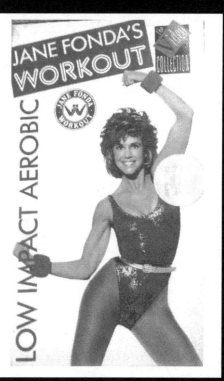

What's On Telly?

Television was a very large part of leisure in the 1980s and with the massive growth in video recorders, the whole family had more control over what they watched and when they watched it.

It was the decade when the huge American 'soaps' **Dallas** and **Dynasty** dominated the ratings and influenced popular debate as well as fashions. In Britain there was a rash of police dramas and the introduction of female detectives in both BBC **'Juliet Bravo'** and ITV **'The Gentle Touch'**. They also covered the land, **'Taggart'** in Scotland, **'Bergerac'** in Jersey, **'The Chinese Detective'** in London and **'Inspector Morse'** in Oxford.

Channel 4 launched in 1982 with its first programme being **'Countdown',** Breakfast TV began in 1983, in 1980s television produced 'historic' shared experiences, **'Who Shot JR'** in Dallas watched by 80 million, the finale of **MASH**, 'Goodbye, Farewell and Amen', by more than 100 million, 30 million tuned in to watch 'Dirty Den' serve his wife 'Angie' with the divorce papers in East Enders and 27 million watched the episode after Alan Bradley tried to kill Rita Fairclough in **Coronation Street.**

What Was New?

Whilst the 80s made huge advances in technology for leisure, Game Boy and Nintendo, VCRs and CDs, disposable cameras and brick shaped mobile phones too, there were other innovations.

In the 'yuppie' years of 'spend, spend, spend', the first smart chip-enabled credit cards were busy being swiped for BMX bikes, Trivial Pursuit and Rubik's Cubes.

Nike told us to 'Just Do It' and we wondered how we'd ever managed without Post-It Notes and disposable contact lenses.

What the world did not want however, was New Coke. Coca Cola changed their classic formula for a sweeter one which received an extremely poor response.

It was one of the worst marketing blunders ever because for the public, this tampered recipe 'Just wasn't it!'. The company brought back the original Coke and sold this new formula as the 'New Coke' till the early 90s.

MUSIC

1980 - 1984

1980   Johnny Logan won the Eurovision Song Contest for Ireland with **What's Another Year** and was No 1 in the UK charts for two weeks in May. He won again in 1987 with **Hold Me Now**.
Abba had their first No 1 of the year with **Winner Takes it All** followed in November with **Super Trouper**.

1981   Two singles stayed at the top of the charts for 5 weeks each this year. First Adam and the Ants with **Stand and Deliver** and in December, The Human League with **Don't You Want Me** which was also the best-selling single of the year.

1982   The year's best seller was Dexey's Midnight Runners and **Come on Eileen**, their second No 1 in the UK. The words express the feelings of an adolescent dreaming of being free from the strictures of a Catholic society and sounded unlike the other hits of the era, no synthesiser, but a banjo, accordion, fiddle and saxophone.

1983   **Karma Chameleon** by the 'New Romantic' band, Culture Club, fronted by singer Boy George, whose androgynous style of dressing caught the attention of the public and the media, became the second Culture Club single to reach No 1 and stayed there for six weeks, also becoming the best-selling single of the year.

1984 **Two Tribes**, the anti-war song by the Liverpool band, Frankie Goes to Hollywood, was a phenomenal success helped by a wide range of remixes and supported by an advertising campaign depicting the band as members of the Red Army. It entered the charts at No 1 and stayed there for nine consecutive weeks, making it the the longest-running No 1 single of the decade.

1985 - 1989

1985   The best seller this year was **The Power of Love** sung by Jennifer Rush. No 1 for five weeks, Rush became the first female artist ever to have a million-selling single in the UK.
Wham and George Michael, having had three No 1's last year, **Wake Me Up Before You Go-Go, Careless Whisper** and **Freedom**, managed only one this year, **I'm Your Man.**

1986   Holiday disco songs such as **Agadoo**, topped the charts for three weeks.
The Christmas No 1 spot was held for four weeks by a reissue, three years after his death, of Jackie Wilson's **Reet Petite (The Sweetest Girl in Town).**

1987   Two singles stayed at No 1 for five weeks, the best-selling of the year, **Never Gonna Give You Up** by Rick Astley and **China in Your Hand** by T'Pau, Carol Decker's group named after the character in Star Trek.

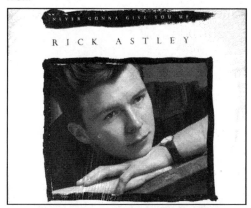

1988   Already known from the Australian soap opera, 'Neighbours', Kylie Minogue burst into the UK charts with **I Should Be So Lucky** from her debut studio album. The song became a worldwide hit.
Cliff Richard was back at No 1 after quite a break, with **Mistletoe and Wine** for the Christmas market.

1989   It was a good year for the Australian golden couple, Jason Donovan and Kylie Minogue. One No 1 together, **Especially For You,** two for Jason, **Too Many Broken Hearts** and **Sealed With a Kiss**, and one for Kylie, **Hand on Your Heart.**
Ride on Time from the debut album by Italian house music group, Black Box, topped the charts for six weeks and sold the most copies of the year.

In The 1980s

Charity Fund Raisers

The 80's saw many 'not for profit' Charity Singles, the best-known being Bob Geldorf and Midge Ure's 'Band Aid' and then 'Live Aid', formed to raise money for famine relief in Ethiopia, who released **Do They Know Its Christmas**, for the first time, in December 1984. It stayed at the top of the charts for five weeks and was the best-selling record of the decade having been released again in 1989.

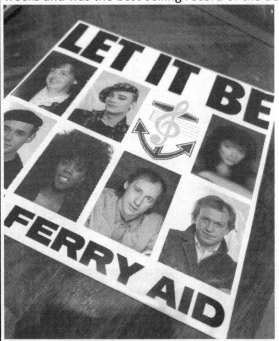

A less well-known charity, 'Ferry Aid', recorded the Beatles' song, **Let It Be** in 1987. This followed the sinking of the ferry 'Ms Herald of the Free' at Zeebrugge, killing 193 passengers and crew. The recording was organised by The Sun newspaper, after it had sold cheap tickets for the ferry on that day.

Tears For Fears, Duran Duran and Simple Minds got together and released **Everybody Wants to Rule the World** in 1986 in support of 'Sport Aid', a campaign to help tackle famine in Africa.

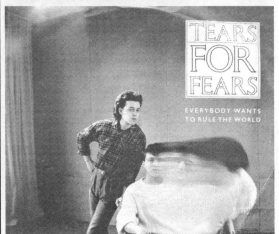

In 1983, Michael Jackson redefined the style, course, and possibilities of music videos. He released **Thriller** and made recording history. The album spent thirty-seven weeks at No 1 on the US Billboard chart. By early 1984, thirty million copies had been sold, and it was still selling at a rate of more than a million copies a week worldwide.

The Compact Disc

In 1981, Kieran Prendiville on BBC's 'Tomorrow's World', demonstrated the CD and wondered, "Whether or not there is a market for these discs, remains to be seen." Well, on the 25th anniversary of its first public release in 1982, it was estimated that 200 billion CDs had been sold worldwide so I guess the answer was "Yes"!

At the end of the 70's, Philips and Sony had teamed up to begin working on CDs for the public and decided on a thin, shiny and circular storage disc, which could hold about 80 minutes of music. The disc had a diameter of 120mm, Sony having insisted that the longest musical performance, Beethoven's entire 9th Symphony at 74 minutes, should fit. A CD could hold an immense amount of data, much more than the vinyl record or the cassette and was perfectly portable.

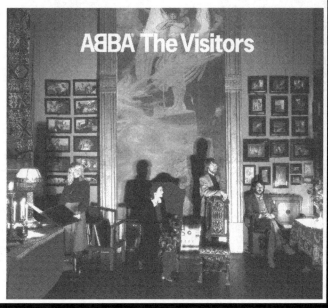

The first commercial CD to be pressed was **Visitors** by Abba, followed quickly by the first album, Billy Joel's **52nd Street**. The biggest selling CD of all time is the Eagles 1976 **Their Greatest Hits** album, which has sold over 38 million copies.

UFOs in the Forest

On 26 December 1980, several US Airforce personnel stationed near the east gate at RAF Woodbridge, reported they had seen "lights" apparently descending into nearby Rendlesham Forest. They initially thought it was a downed aircraft but, upon investigation, they saw what they described as a glowing object, metallic in appearance, with coloured lights.

After daybreak on the morning of December 27, servicemen returned to a small clearing in the forest and found three small impressions on the ground in a triangular pattern, as well as burn marks and broken branches on nearby trees.

The 'Rendlesham Forest Incident' made headline news and theories suggest it was either an actual alien visitation, a secret military aircraft, a misinterpretation of natural lights, the beam of Orfordness Lighthouse, or just a hoax.

In The 1980s

Mount St Helens

In March 1980 a series of volcanic explosions began at Mount St Helens, Washington in the US, culminating in a major explosive eruption on May 18. The eruption column rose 80,000 feet (15 miles) into the atmosphere and deposited ash over 11 states and into some Canadian provinces. At the same time, snow, ice, and entire glaciers on the volcano melted, forming a series of large volcanic mudslides that reached as far as 50 miles to the southwest. Thermal energy released during the eruption was equal to 26 megatons of TNT.

Regarded as the most significant and disastrous volcanic eruption in the country's history, about 57 people were killed, hundreds of square miles were reduced to wasteland, thousands of animals were killed, and Mount St. Helens was left with a crater on its north side. The area is now preserved as the Mount St Helens National Volcanic Monument.

One day before the eruption and several months afterwards. About a third of the mountain was blown away.

SPORT

1980 - 1984

1980 Eight days after the **Boston marathon**, Rosie Ruiz, a Cuban American, is disqualified as the winner 'in the fastest time ever run by a woman'. Investigations found that she did not run the entire course, joining about a half-mile before the finish.

Larry Holmes defeats Muhammed Ali to retain boxing's **WBC World Heavyweight** title. It is Ali's last world title bout.

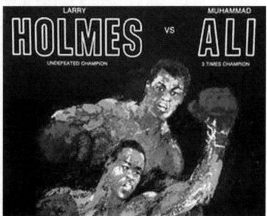

1981 At **Wimbledon**, John McEnroe defeats Björn Borg to gain his 3rd career Grand Slam title and his 1st Wimbledon title.

In the ladies' final, Chris Evert Lloyd defeats Hana Mandlíková to gain her 12th career Grand Slam title and her third and last Wimbledon title.

1982 In June, at Pebble Beach, the American Tom Watson wins **The US Open** and a month later, at Royal Troon, he wins the **The Open.** He is only the third golfer, at that time, to win both Championships in the same year.

In Spain, Italy defeat West Germany in the **World Cup Final.** The tournament features the first penalty shoot-out in the World Cup competition.

1983 The **FA Cup** is won by Manchester United who, having drawn the first final with Brighton and Hove Albion, win the replay, 4-0.

1984 John McEnroe has his best season. He wins 13 singles tournaments, including **Wimbledon** where he loses just one set on his way to his third Wimbledon singles title. This includes a straight set win over Jimmy Connors in the final. He also wins the **US Open**, capturing the year-end number one ranking.

1985 - 1989

1985 Ireland is the championship winner in the **Rugby Five Nations** winning their tenth solo title, but it would prove to be their last for 24 years, until their Grand Slam in 2009.

Alain Prost becomes the **F1 World Champion** Driver, winning five of the sixteen Grand Prix. The first ever world championship **Australian Grand Prix** is held on a street circuit in Adelaide.

1986 In the **World Cup**, Argentina wins by defeating West Germany 3-2. Diego Maradona is the biggest star of the event, and his 'Hand of God' goal is well remembered. The event also sees the introduction of the 'Mexican Wave'.

1987 In **Cricket** the Indian opening batsman, Sunil Gavaskar reaches 10,000 test runs to become the first ever player to score this many. In the **Cricket World Cup** played for the first time outside Britain, in India, Australia win by defeating their arch-rivals, England.

1988 The **FA Cup** is won by Wimbledon FC's 'Crazy Gang', who defeat league champions Liverpool through a headed goal by Lawrie Sanchez. This is Wimbledon's only FA Cup title during its lifetime.

1989 On heavy, almost un-raceable ground, the iconic grey Desert Orchid, ridden by Simon Sherwood, in a race that defined his illustrious career, wins the **Cheltenham Gold Cup**. In 2005 this was voted the 'Greatest Race of All Time' by Racing Post readers.

In The 1980s

You cannot be serious!

During the 1981 Wimbledon Championships, John McEnroe uttered what has become the most immortal phrase in tennis, if not all sport, when he screamed "you cannot be serious" at a Wimbledon umpire while disputing a line call. Already called "Superbrat" by the British tabloid press for his verbal volleys during previous Wimbledon matches, it was in a first-round match against fellow American Tom Gullikson, who was serving at 15-30 and 1-1 in the first set when a McEnroe shot was called out. Approaching the umpire, he said: "Chalk came up all over the place, you can't be serious man." Then, his anger rising, he bawled the words that would stay with him for a lifetime and find its way into the sporting annals. "You cannot be serious," he screamed. "That ball was on the line".

On the receiving end of the tirade was umpire Edward James, who eventually responded by politely announcing: "I'm going to award a point against you Mr McEnroe." It made little difference, McEnroe went on to win in straight sets and two weeks later had his final victory over Bjorn Borg.

Torvill and Dean

On Valentine's Day 1984, Jayne Torvill and Christopher Dean made history at the Winter Olympics in Sarajevo and set a new standard for world class figure skating. The duo from Nottingham, were the last to perform in their category and their performance, self-choreographed to 4½ minutes of Ravel's Bolero, was seamless, elegant and hypnotic. As they sank to the ice in the dramatic finale, the whole stadium stood and applauded. Their dance had captured the world's imagination and won Gold. The unanimous scores of 6.0 for artistic impression made them the highest-scoring figure skaters of all time.

Their routine, made Ravel's Boléro with its steady crescendo and repeated snare-drum rhythms, synonymous with figure-skating.

British Car Manufacturing

Gallery:

The 1980s was still a busy period for British car manufacturers and many of the bestselling cars of the decade were made in Britain.
The top 10 cars were:
1. Ford Escort
2. Vauxhall Cavalier
3. Ford Fiesta
4. Austin Metro
5. Ford Sierra (which replaced the
6. Ford Cortina)
6. Vauxhall Astra
7. Ford Orion
8. Austin Maestro
9. Vauxhall Nova
10. Ford Grenada

However the list of the **'Most influential Cars of the 1980s'** shows how the British car industry was soon to be decimated. The list includes:
Audi Quatrro; Porsche 944: Renault Scenic; Mercedes 190; BMW 3 Series; VW Golf; Volvo 240 Estate; Peugeot 205 and the Toyota Carolla.

The Ford Cortina was replaced by the Ford Sierra in 1982

The Ford Fiesta has been ever popular right up to the present day.

The Austin Metro was the replacement for the mini.

The VW Golf had front wheel drive and built a reputation for quality and reliability

The Porsche 944 was the choice of the newly rich 'yuppies' of the 1980s

Clunk Click Every Trip

Although car manufacturers had been obliged to install seatbelts since 1965, it was not until January 1983 that the law requiring all drivers to wear their belts came into force. In spite of a great deal of 'grumbling' and more, ranging from *"the erosion of our civil liberties, another example of the Nanny State"*, to *"its uncomfortable, restrictive and creases my clothes"* and horror stories of crash victims being *"hanged"* by their belts or suffering greater injury, 90% of drivers and front seat passengers were observed to be wearing seat belts soon after the law came into effect – and these rates have been sustained since then. There was an immediate 25% reduction in driver fatalities and a 29 per cent reduction in fatal injuries among front seat passengers.

In 1989 it became compulsory for all children under 14 to wear a seat belt in the rear and when seatbelt wearing became compulsory for all rear-seat occupants in 1991, there was an immediate increase from 10% to 40% in observed seat belt wearing rates.

IN THE 1980s

Aviation

When Airbus designed the A300 during the late 1960s and early 1970s, it envisaged a broad family of airliners with which to compete against Boeing and Douglas, the two established US aerospace manufacturers.

The launch of the A320 in 1987 guaranteed the status of Airbus as a major player in the aircraft market – the aircraft had over 400 orders before it first flew.

Motorcycles

Only 3000 Honda FVR750R motorcycles were made, race bred machines with lights thrown on to make them road legal and sold to the public. The first batch of 1000 sold out instantly. With a top speed of 153mph the V-four powered RC30 was one of the fastest sports bike of the decade but it was the track proven frame that meant it handled like a genuine racer. It also had a soundtrack to die for and was absolutely beautiful.

The Docklands Light Railway

The Docklands Light Railway was first opened in August 1987 as an automated, light metro system to serve the redeveloped Docklands area of London as a cheap public transport solution. The original network comprised two routes - Tower Gateway to Island Gardens and Stratford to Island Gardens and was mainly elevated on disused railway viaducts, new concrete viaducts and disused surface railway tracks. The trains were fully automated, controlled by computer, and had no driver.

They did however have a "Train Captain" who was responsible for patrolling the train, checking tickets, making announcements and controlling the doors. They could take control of the train should there be an equipment failure or emergency. The first generation of rolling stock comprised eleven lightweight units and the stations, mostly of a common design, constructed from standard components and usually featuring a short half-cylindrical, glazed, blue canopy, were designed specifically for these single articulated trains. The 15 stations were all above ground and needed no staff.

THE MAJOR NEWS STORIES

1990 - 1994

1990:
Feb: Nelson Mandela is released from prison in South Africa, after 27 years behind bars.

Nov: Margaret Thatcher resigns as Prime Minister. At 11 years, she was the longest serving PM of the 20th Century.

1991:
Jan: The Gulf War begins, as the Royal Air Force joins Allied aircraft in bombing raids on Iraq

Apr: After a year of protests and riots, the government confirms that the Poll Tax is to be replaced by a new Council Tax in 1993.

1992:
Apr: At the General Election the Conservative Party are re-elected for a fourth term under John Major.

Nov: Part of Windsor Castle is gutted in a fire causing millions of pounds worth of damage and The Queen describes this year as an Annus Horribilis.

1993:
Apr: The Queen announces that Buckingham Palace will open to the public for the first time

Sep: The UK Independence Party which supports the breakaway from the EU is formed.

Dec: Diana, Princess of Wales. withdraws from public life.

1994:
Mar: The Church of England ordains its first female priests.

May: The Channel Tunnel between Britain and France is officially opened.

Nov: The first UK National Lottery draw takes place.

1992: The 'Maastricht Treaty' was concluded between the 'then' twelve member states of the European Communities. This foundation treaty of the EU announced a new stage in the process of European integration, shared citizenship and a single currency. There were two headquarters, one in Brussels and one in Strasbourg,

1991: The internet already existed but no one had thought of a way of how to link one document directly to another until in 1989, British scientist Tim Berners-Lee, invented the WorldWideWeb. The www. was introduced in 1991 as the first web browser and the first website went online in August.

1995 - 1999

1997: The UK transfers sovereignty of Hong Kong, the largest remaining British colony, to the People's Republic of China as the 99 years lease on the territory formally ends.

1999: On 1st January, the new European currency, the Euro is launched and some 320 million people from eleven European countries begin carrying the same money in their wallets.
Britain's Labour government preferred to stay with the pound sterling instead.

1995:

Feb: Barings Bank, the UK's oldest merchant bank, collapses after rogue trader Nick Leeson loses $1.4 billion.

Apr: All telephone area dialling codes are changed in the UK.

Aug: Pubs in England are permitted to remain open throughout Sunday afternoon.

1996:

Feb: The Prince and Princess of Wales agree to divorce more than three years after separating.

Jul: Dolly the Sheep becomes the first mammal to be successfully cloned from an adult cell.

1997:

May: Tony Blair wins a landslide General Election for the Labour Party.

Aug: Princess Diana is killed in a car crash in Paris. Dodi Fayed, the heir to the Harrods empire is killed with her

1998:

Mar: Construction on the Millenium Dome begins. It will be the centre piece for a national celebration.

Apr: The Good Friday Agreement between the UK and Irish governments is signed.

1999:

Apr: A minimum wage is introduced in the UK – set at £3.60 an hour for workers over 21, and £3 for workers under 21

Jun: Construction of the Millenium Dome is finished and in October, the London Eye begins to be lifted into position.

THE HOME

Home life in the 1990s was changing again. Family time was not cherished as it had once been, children had a lot more choice and were becoming more independent with their own TVs programmes, personal computers, music systems, mobile phones and, crucially, the introduction of the world wide web, which meant life would never be the same again.

After school and weekend organised activities for the young burgeoned, with teenagers able to take advantage of the fast-food chains, or eating at different times, meaning no more family eating together. Families 'lived in separate' rooms, there were often two televisions so different channels could be watched and children wanted to play with their Nintendos or listen to their Walkmans in their own rooms. Their rooms were increasingly themed, from Toy Story to Athena posters, a ceiling full of sticker stars that illuminated a room with their green glow and somewhere in the house, room had to be made for the computer desk.

Track lighting was an easy way to illuminate a room without relying on multiple lamps and it became a popular feature in many '90s homes along with corner baths — most of which also had a water jet function which suddenly turned your bath into a low-budget jacuzzi!

IN THE 1990s

In 1990, 68% of UK households owned at least one car, and the use of 'out of town' supermarkets and shopping centres, where just about anything and everything could be purchased in the same area, meant that large weekly or even monthly shops could be done in a single outing and combined with the huge increase in domestic freezers and ready prepared foods, time spent in the kitchen and cooking could be greatly reduced.

Over 80% of households owned a washing machine and 50%, a tumble dryer, so the need to visit the laundrette all but disappeared and instead of "Monday is washing day", the family's laundry could be carried out on an 'as and when' basis. All contributing to an increase in leisure time.

Nearly three-quarters of homes had microwave cookers and for working women who did not want to do their own cleaning, Merry Maids set up their home cleaning franchise in the UK in 1990 and many other companies followed suit.

Commuting
In Great Britain at the beginning of the 1990s, the *average* one-way commute to work was 38 minutes in London, 33 minutes in the south-east, and 21 minutes in the rest of the country. By the end of the decade, full-time workers commuting to and from London, had lost an additional 70 minutes per week of home time to commuting but, by contrast, outside the south-east of Britain, there was no increase in commuting time over the decade. In the south-east, 30% of workers took at least 45 minutes to get to work. In the rest of the country, only 10% did.

ART AND CULTURE

1990 - 1994

1990 In Rome, on the eve of the final of the FIFA World Cup, the Three Tenors sing together for the first time. The event is broadcast live and watched worldwide by millions of people. The highlight is Luciano Pavarotti's performance of Nessun Dorma.
The first Hampton Court Palace Flower Show takes place.

1991 Dame Margot Fonteyn, the Royal Ballet's Prima Ballerina, dies in Panama City, exactly 29 years after her premiere with Rudolf Nureyev who made his debut in 'Giselle'.

1992 Damien Hirst's "Shark", featuring a preserved shark, is first shown at an exhibition at the Saatchi Gallery in London.
Under the new Further and Higher Education Act, Polytechnics are allowed to become new Universities and award degrees of their own.
The last edition of Punch, the UK's oldest satirical magazine since 1841, is published.

1993 Bookmakers cut their odds on the monarchy being abolished by the year 2000 from 100 to 1 to 50 to 1.
QVC launches the first television shopping channel in the UK.

1994 The Duchess of Kent joins the Roman Catholic Church, the first member of the Royal Family to convert to Catholicism for more than 300 years.
The Sunday Trading Act comes into full effect, permitting retailers to trade on Sundays but restricts larger stores to a maximum of six hours, between 10 am and 6 pm.

1995 - 1999

1995 The first ever World Book Day was held on 23rd April, picked to celebrate the anniversary of William Shakespeare's death.

The BBC begins regular Digital Audio Broadcasting from Crystal Palace.

1996 Shortly after publication of the Italian edition of his book 'The Art Forger's Handbook', English-born art forger, Eric Hebborn is beaten to death in Rome.
The Stone of Scone is installed in Edinburgh Castle 700 years after it was removed from Scotland by King Edward I of England.

1997 The Teletubbies caused a sensation when they appeared on BBC TV. They were the most sought-after toy of the year.
The reconstruction of the Elizabethan Globe Theatre, called Shakespeare's Globe opens in London with a production of Shakespeare's 'Henry V'.

1998 Britain's largest sculpture, the Angel of the North by Anthony Gormley is installed at Low Eighton, Gateshead.
More than 15,000 people attend a tribute concert held for Diana, Princess of Wales, at her family home, Althorp Park.

1999 The children's picture book, 'The Gruffalo' by Julia Donaldson is first published.

Media coverage for the Turner Prize was dominated by extreme critical response to Tracey Emin's work 'My Bed' – an installation of her unmade bed, complete with dirty sheets and detritus.

1997: 'Harry Potter and the Philosopher's Stone' by JK Rowling made its debut in June. The initial edition of this first book in the series, comprised 500 copies and the novel has gone on to sell in excess of 120 million. The success of the whole Harry Potter phenomenon is well known, and there have been less expected benefits too. Certainly, before the films, children loved reading the books and boosted the reported numbers of children reading and indeed, reading longer books.

The perception of boarding schools, often associated with misery and cruel, spartan regimes was changed for some by Hogwarts School of Witchcraft and Wizardry. The sense of excitement, community and friendship of the children, the camaraderie of eating together and playing together, made going away to school more appealing for many.

The amazing visual effects used in the films were instrumental in persuading Hollywood to consider UK technical studios and raised the number of visual effects Oscar nominations for British companies significantly.

1997: The Guggenheim Museum of modern and contemporary art, designed by Canadian-American architect Frank Gehry, opened in Bilbao. The building represents an architectural landmark of innovating design, a spectacular structure.

The museum was originally a controversial project. Bilbao's industry, steel and shipbuilding was dying, and the city decided to regenerate to become a modern technological hub of the Basque region, and the controversy was, instead of an office block or factory, the centre piece would be a brand-new art gallery.

It is a spectacular building, more like a sculpture with twisted metal, glass, titanium and limestone, a futuristic setting for fine works of art. The gamble paid off, in the first twenty years, the museum attracted more than 19 million visitors with 70% from outside Spain. Foreign tourists continue to travel through the Basque country bringing a great economic boost to the region and Bilbao itself, has transformed from a grimy post-industrial town to a tourist hotspot.

FILMS

1990 - 1994

1990 It was Oscar time for an epic western this year and **Dances With Wolves**, directed and starring Kevin Costner with seven Academy Awards, won Best Picture and Best Director. It is one of only three Westerns to win the Oscar for Best Picture, the other two being **Cimmaron** in 1931 and **Unforgotten** in **1992**.

1991 *"Well, Clarice - have the lambs stopped screaming?"* wrote Dr Hannibal Lecter to the young FBI trainee, Clarice Starling. The thriller, **The Silence of the Lambs**, about a cannibalistic serial killer, scared audiences half to death and won the Best Picture Award.

1992 The nominations for the Academy Awards held some serious themes. **The Crying Game** was set against the backdrop of the 'troubles' in Northern Ireland. There was a blind retired Army officer in **Scent of a Woman**, rising troubles in colonial French Vietnam in **Indochine** and the invasion of Panama in **The Panama Deception**.

1993 The acclaimed **Schindler's List** won Best Picture with stiff competition from **The Piano** which won Best Original Screenplay and Robin Williams as **Mrs Doubtfire** which became the second highest grossing film of the year.

1994 Disney's animated musical **The Lion King** made the most money this year, but **Forest Gump** took the prize for Best Picture. The British film **Four Weddings and a Funeral** was a huge success and brought WH Auden's beautiful poem 'Funeral Blues' into the limelight.

1995 - 1999

1995 The tense, amazingly technically correct, story of the ill-fated **Apollo 13** quest to land on the moon failed to win the top Oscar, beaten by Mel Gibson in **Braveheart**, the American take on the story of William Wallace and the first Scottish war of independence against England.

1996 The English Patient a romantic war drama won the Best Picture, up against Mike Leigh's **Secrets and Lies** which won the Best British Film.

1997 The blockbuster **Titanic** was the film of the year. The combination of romance and disaster proving irresistible. Harland & Wolfe, the builders of RMS Titanic shared blueprints they thought were lost with the crew to produce the scale models, computer-generated imagery and a reconstruction of the ship itself, to re-create the sinking.

1998 Shakespeare in Love, a fictional love affair between Shakespeare and Viola de Lesseps whilst he is writing Romeo and Juliet was hugely popular and won seven Oscars.

1999 In **American Beauty,** Kevin Spacey plays Lester Burnham, an unhappy executive whose midlife awakening is the crux of the story. Bad as he thinks his life is, he cannot not stop seeing the beauty of the world around him.

**"Fear can hold you prisoner,
Hope can set you free."**

In 1994, Tim Robbins and Morgan Freeman starred **The Shawshank Redemption**, an inspirational, life-affirming and uplifting, old-fashioned style prison film and character study in the ilk of 'The Birdman of Alcatraz'. Set in a fictional, oppressive Shawshank State Prison in Maine, two imprisoned men bond over the years, in a tale of friendship, patience, hope, survival and ultimately finding solace and eventual redemption through acts of common decency.

The film was initially a box office disappointment. Many reasons were put forward for its failure at the time, including a general unpopularity of prison films, its lack of female characters and even the title, which was considered to be confusing. However, it was nominated for seven Academy Awards, failed to win a single Oscar, but this raised awareness and increased the film's popularity such that it is now preserved in the US National Film Registry as "culturally, historically, or aesthetically significant".

The Full Monty

In 1997 whilst huge audiences were crying over Kate Winslet and Leonardo di Caprio in **Titanic,** equally huge audiences were laughing at the story of six unemployed men in Sheffield, four of them former steel workers, who are in dire need of cash and who decide to emulate 'The Chippendales' dance, striptease troupe. They devise a dance act with their difference being, that Gaz decides their show must be even better than the originals and declares to the friends that they will go 'the full Monty' – they will strip all the way. Although primarily a comedy, the film touches on several serious subjects too, including unemployment, father's rights – Gaz is unable to pay maintenance to his estranged wife and she is seeking sole custody of his son – and working-class culture, depression and suicide. The film was a huge success as it ultimately is about humanity and the problems people all over the world struggle with.

FASHION

SUPERMODELS

The original supermodels of the 1980s, Linda Evangelista, Naomi Campbell, Christy Turlington and Cindy Crawford were joined later by Claudia Schiffer and then Kate Moss to become the "Big Six". Models used to be categorised as 'print' or 'runway' but the "Big Six" showed that they could do it all, catwalk, print campaigns, magazine covers and even music videos and they became pop 'icons' in their own right. The models were also known for their earning capacity, one famous remark from Linda Evangelista, "We don't wake up for less than $10,000 a day!"

But with the popularity of grunge, came a shift away from the fashion for feminine curves and wholesome looking women, and in came the rise of a new breed of fragile, individual-looking and often younger, models, epitomised by Kate Moss. Her waif-like thinness and delicacy complemented the unkempt look that was popular in the early nineties and a new phrase 'heroin chic' described the down-at-heel settings for fashion shoots presented in magazines. By the end of the decade however, attitudes had shifted and concern about the health of the skeletal model was becoming a source of great debate.

GOTH

During the mid to late 1990s, the sub-culture of gothic fashion peaked in popularity. Their distinguishing features were black, antiquated and homogeneous features. Long black hair, black eyeliner, black nail polish, silver jewellery and face piercings teamed with long, black leather coats worn over frilly shirts and tight black trousers or even fetish wear. Girls often wore corsets, lace gloves and short leather skirts, velvets and fishnets with accessories often borrowed from the punk fashion such as spiked wristbands and chokers.

Siouxsie Sioux was particularly influential, since her gig at Futurama in 1980 she had been influencing how the music with the Banshees, would dress and she may well have been inspired by Theda Bara, the 1910s silent film, femme fatale, renowned for her dark eyeshadow and 'Vamp' look.

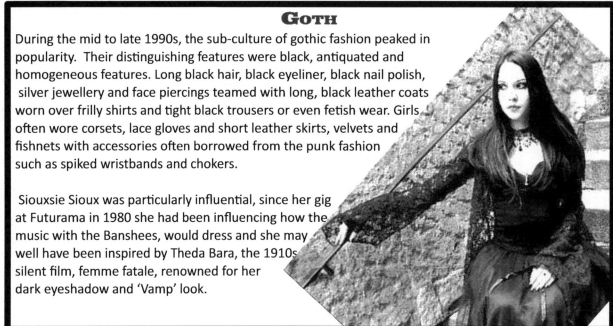

In The 1990s

Grunge

Grunge was a style for the young that emerged in Seattle in the late 1980s and by the early 90s had spread across the world. Made popular by bands such as Nirvana, it was a fashion for both men and women. The look was simple, an oversized flannel shirt, sometimes worn over a t-shirt, and baggy, worn out jeans to give an overall, dishevelled, appearance. The clothes were found ideally in charity shops or at the back of "Dad's wardrobe". A pair of Doc Martens or Converse shoes finished the ensemble.

Nirvana's lead singer Kurt Cobain epitomised the look with holes in his jeans and cardigan sweaters and the fashion world caught on when their second album, 'Nevermind' was released in 1991 and grunge made it onto the catwalk – specifically by Calvin Klein on an 18-year-old Kate Moss. Shrunken baby doll dresses, old prom dresses or even old petticoats and simple slip dresses appeared, often worn with chunky boots and for men, beanies, band t-shirts and knitted sweaters with patterns.

Friends

For women, long loose hair was the most popular women's style, but the most requested hairstyle of the 1990s was said to be 'The Rachel'. Jennifer Anniston's character in 'Friends', Rachel Green, had the haircut people wanted – bouncy, layered, shoulder length, obviously styled to within an inch of its life yet at the same time artfully tousled.

Hoodies

Utilitarian styles such as cargo pants and The Gap's hooded sweatshirts became popular for everyday wear. Industrial and military styles crept into mainstream fashion and camouflage pants were everywhere on the street.

There was also a concerted move towards logoed clothing such as by Tommy Hilfiger

LEISURE

THE GAMES CHILDREN PLAYED

The trend in the 90s was for more electronic, video and computer games but younger children still enjoyed many of the traditional past-times, and events in the 90s such as the FIFA World Cups and the Olympics, produced special collections which reignited interest in collecting 'stickers,' and filling albums.

Crazes were still all the craze too and it was digital pets like Tamagotchi, housed in their small, egg-shaped, handheld video game console that became the biggest fads of the end of the decade.

The Teletubbies caused a huge sensation in 1997, communicating through gibberish and designed to resemble real-life toddlers, they became a huge commercial success, the toy Teletubbies being the most demanded toy of 1997.

However, it was Sony's PlayStation which was the big innovation of the 90s. The first version was able to process games stored on CD-ROMs and introduced 3D graphics to the industry. It had a low retail price and Sony employed aggressive youth marketing. Ridge Racer was the classic motor racing game used in the launch and the popularity of this game was crucial to the early success of the PlayStation.

RESTORATION OF THE SPA

From being at the centre of society in previous times, the spa industry had declined so much that by the 50s, leading spas such as those at Buxton, Cheltenham and Tunbridge Wells had closed. The 1990s saw a simultaneous rise of increasing disposable wealth, and the popularity of a new concept of the spa, pure self-indulgence and pampering.

The need to pause and detox from time to time fitted nicely into the growth of a 'wellness' culture and the understanding of holistic wellbeing, treatments to soothe the mind, body and spirit. Wearing a luxurious white robe and slippers, lounging by a heated pool reading magazines and dipping from time to time into the whirlpools, a trip to the steam room or sauna before taking a light lunch and then unwinding to a fragranced oil body massage because, as L'Oreal had been saying since the 70s, "you're worth it!"

IN THE 1990s

WHERE WE WENT ON HOLIDAY

In the 90s, if we went on a foreign holiday at all, 26m of us in 1996, the norm was to go for just the one, two-week summer break. Booking with a Travel Agent in town or finding a cheap package deal on Teletext, we arrived at our destination with a guide-book, Travellers Cheques and a camera complete with film.

Our favourite places were Spain and France, many of us travelling on the cross-Channel ferries rather than on the budget airlines. Our other favourite hot spots were Belgium, Turkey, Egypt, Kenya and Tunisia.

Although the gap year began in the 1960s, it was in the 1990s when the idea became the 'thing to do' amongst the children of the new wealthy middle classes.

Many visited India, Pakistan and Nepal, Australia, Thailand, the USA and New Zealand being their favoured countries to visit.

Some did voluntary work in the developing nations, building schools and teaching children English.

The 90s saw plenty of new cruise ships being launched for what became a massive growth industry. New cruise lines were formed, and many existing lines merged and Royal Caribbean, Celebrity, Fred Olsen and Carnival, Disney, Silver Sea and Princess lines were all introducing, predominantly older people, to new places and entertaining them royally on the way.

For others, at the opposite end of the cruising scale, was the immensely popular, 'Booze Cruise'. The day trip across the channel to France to stock up on duty free wine and cigarettes.

MUSIC

1990 - 1994

1990 Elton John's **Sacrifice** was initially released as a single in 1989 but only reached No. 55 in the UK. In mid-1990, Radio 1 DJ, Steve Wright began playing it and it soon caught on with other DJs and when re-released as a double A-side single with **Healing Hands** it became John's first solo No 1 single remaining at the top for five weeks.

1991 Cher made the 1960s **Shoop Shoop Song (It's in His Kiss)** an international hit once again. **(Everything I Do) I Do It for You**, from the soundtrack of the film 'Robin Hood: Prince of Thieves' was sung by Bryan Adams and became a huge hit, the best-selling single of the year and stayed at No 1 for 16 weeks.

1992 Shakespeares Sister had their only No 1 UK single hit with **Stay** which stayed at the top for eight consecutive weeks.
The best-selling single of the year was Whitney Houston singing the song written by Dolly Parton, **I Will Always Love You.**

1993 **Pray** by Take That, written by Gary Barlow, was the first of twelve singles by the band to reach No 1 in the UK and the first of a run of four consecutive No 1's.

I'd Do Anything for Love (But I Won't Do That) was the song of the year and won Meat Loaf a Grammy Award for the Best Rock Solo Vocal Performance.

1994 The Most Beautiful Girl in the World by the unpronounceable Love Symbol, or 'The Artist Formerly Known as Prince' reached No 1.
The Manchester United football squad had the help of Status Quo, who wrote and sang along on their two week No 1 hit, **Come on You Reds.**

1995 - 1999

1995 Four artists had two No 1 hits this year. The Outhere Brothers with **Don't Stop (Wiggle Wiggle)** and **Boom Boom Boom**. Take That with **Back for Good** and **Never Forget** and Robson Green & Jerome Flynn with **Unchained Melody/ Bluebirds Over the White Cliffs of Dover** – the best seller of the year, and **I Believe/Up On the Roof.**

1996 This was a year with 23 No 1s. Most being at the top for only one week, but Fugees was No 1 twice with the same song **Killing Me Softly.** Firstly, for four weeks in June and then with a break for a week for **Three Lions (Football's Coming Home)** and another week in July.

1997 Elton John topped the charts for five weeks with **Candle in the Wind 1997**, a re-written and re-recorded version of **Candle in the Wind** as a tribute to the late Diana, Princess of Wales.
Another kind of tribute, this time to the popularity of the Teletubbies, their **Teletubbies say 'Eh-oh!'** stayed at No 1 for two weeks in December.

1998 The main soundtrack song from the blockbuster film Titanic provided Celine Dion with a hit, **My Heart Will Go On.**
Cher reinvented herself, and her song, **Believe** stayed at No 1 for seven weeks and was the year's best seller.

1999 Britney Spears made her debut single with **...Baby One More Time** which became a worldwide hit and sold over ten million copies.
Cliff Richard's **Millenium Prayer** is knocked off its 3 weeks at No 1 spot just in time for the boy band, Westlife, to make the Christmas No 1 with **I Have a Dream/Seasons in the Sun.**

In The 1990s

Cool Britannia

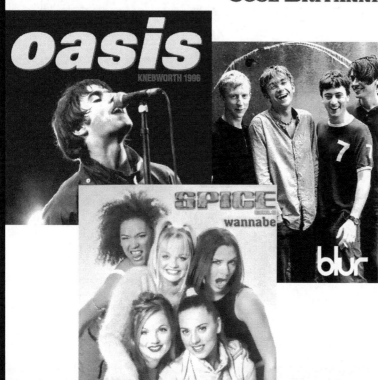

Throughout the mid and second half of the 1990s, Cool Britannia was a period of increased pride in the culture of the UK inspired by the 'Swinging London' of the 1960s pop culture. This brought about a huge success of 'Britpop' with groups such as Blur and Oasis and particularly, the Spice Girls.

Mel B, 'Scary Spice', Melanie C, 'Sporty Spice', Emma Bunton, 'Baby Spice', Geri Halliwell, 'Ginger Spice' and Victoria Beckham, 'Posh Spice' brought girl power to the fore. Their first single was 1996's iconic **Wannabe**, which established the group as a global phenomenon as 'Spice Mania' circled the globe. They scored the Christmas Number 1 single three years in a row and had nine UK No 1's in total.

Love Is All Around

In June 1994, Wet Wet Wet the Scottish soft rock band had a huge international hit, with 15 weeks as the UK No 1, with their cover of the 1960s hit by The Troggs, **Love Is All Around.** Their version was used on the soundtrack of the blockbuster film 'Four Weddings and a Funeral'.

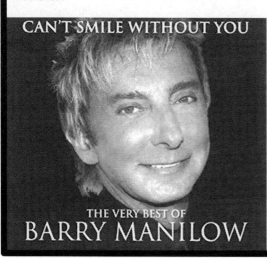

Richard Curtis, the director of the film, had approached Wet Wet Wet with a choice of three cover songs to record for the soundtrack, the other two being **I Will Survive** by Gloria Gaynor and Barry Manilow's **Can't Smile Without You**.

SCIENCE AND NATURE

THE HUBBLE TELESCOPE

The Hubble telescope is a general-purpose orbiting observatory. Orbiting approximately 380 mi (612 km) above Earth, the 12.5-ton Hubble Space Telescope has peered farther into the universe than any telescope before it. The Hubble, which was launched on April 24, 1990, has produced images with unprecedented resolution at visible, near-ultraviolet, and near-infrared wavelengths since its originally faulty optics were corrected in 1993.

Although ground-based telescopes are finally starting to catch up, the Hubble continues to produce a stream of unique observations. During the 1990s and now into the 2000s, the Hubble has revolutionised the science of astronomy, becoming one, if not the most, important instruments ever used in astronomy.

ADD TO BASKET

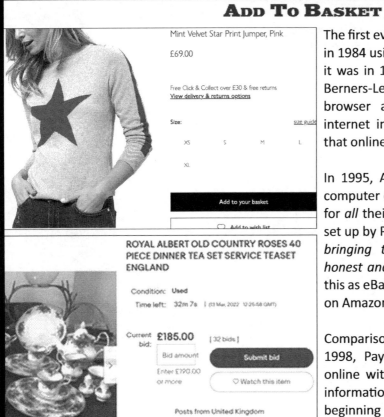

The first ever shopper bought online from Tesco in 1984 using her television remote control, but it was in 1990s, following the creation by Tim Berners-Lee of the World Wide Web server and browser and the commercialisation of the internet in 1991 giving birth to e-commerce, that online shopping really began to take off.

In 1995, Amazon began selling books online, computer companies started using the internet for *all* their transactions and Auction Web was set up by Pierre Omidyar as a site *"dedicated to bringing together buyers and sellers in an honest and open marketplace."* We now know this as eBay and we can buy just about anything on Amazon.

Comparison sites were set up in 1997 and in 1998, PayPal was founded, the way to pay online without having to share your financial information. By 1999, online only shops were beginning to emerge and paved the way for 'Click for Checkout' to become commonplace.

IN THE 1990s

THE KYOTO PROTOCOL

In December 1997, at the instigation of the United Nations, representatives from 160 countries met in Kyoto, Japan, to discuss climate change and draft the Kyoto Protocol which aimed to restrict the greenhouse gas emissions associated with global warming.

The protocol focused on demands that 37 developed nations work to reduce their greenhouse gas emissions placing the burden on developed nations, viewing them as the primary sources and largely responsible for carbon emissions.

Developing nations were asked only to comply voluntarily, exempted from the protocol's requirements. The protocol's approach included establishing a 'carbon credits system' whereby nations can earn credits by participating in emission reduction projects in other nations. A carbon credit is a tradeable permit or certificate that provides the holder

SHOCK WAVES

A large earthquake, by British standards, occurred near Bishop's Castle, Shropshire on the Welsh Borders on 2 April 1990 at 13:46 GMT. With a magnitude of 5.1, the shock waves were felt over a wide area of Britain, from Ayrshire in the north to Cornwall in the south, Kent in the east and Dublin in the west.

Worldwide in 1990, there were 18 quakes of magnitude 7.0 or above and 134 quakes between 6.0 and 7.0, 4435 quakes between 4.0 and 5.0, 2755 quakes between 3.0 and 4.0, and 8618 quakes between 2.0 and 3.0. There were also 29800 quakes below magnitude 2.0 which people don't normally feel.

The strongest quake was north of Pulau Hulawa Island in Indonesia, registering 7.8 on the Richter scale.

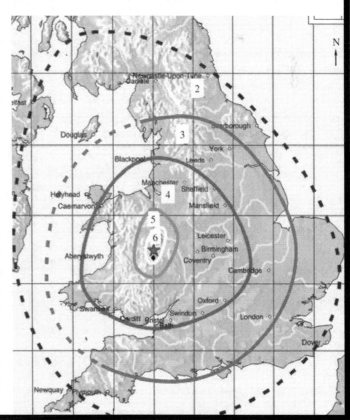

SPORT

1990 - 1994

1990 West Germany won the **FIFA World Cup** in Rome, defeating defending champions Argentina, 1–0 in the final.

The British golfer, Nick Faldo, had an amazing year, winning both the **Masters** and the Claret Jug at the **Open** at St Andrews, and capturing the PGA Player of the Year award, the first non-American to do so.

1991 At the **World Athletics** Championships in Tokyo, Mike Powell broke the 23 year-long world record **long jump** set by Bob Beamon, with a jump of 29' 4½".

1992 The rugby, **Five Nations Championship** is won by England who complete the Grand Slam for the second consecutive year.

The summer **Olympics** are held in Barcelona, Spain where Sally Gunnell takes home gold in the Women's 400 metres hurdles, Linford Christie triumphs in the Men's 100 metres, and rowers Matthew Pinsent and Steve Redgrave finish first in the Men's coxless pair, the first Olympic gold for all four athletes. In the **Paralympics**, Tanni Grey-Thompson in her debut Games, takes home four golds and a silver.

1993 Manchester United win the inaugural **English Premier League** title, their first league title in 26 years.

Shane Warne bowls the so-called 'Ball of the Century' in the first Test at Old Trafford. With his first ball against England, in his first **Ashes**, he bowled Mike Gatting out.

1994 Tiger Woods becomes the youngest man ever to win the **U.S. Amateur Golf Championships**, at age 18.

George Foreman becomes **Boxing's** oldest Heavyweight Champion at forty-five.

1995 - 1999

1995 In motor racing, Michael Schumacher wins his second consecutive **Drivers' Championship**, and Benetton wins its first and only Constructors' Championship.

British triple jumper Jonathan Edwards sets a world record in the **Athletics World Championships**, jumping 60' (18.29 m).

1996 The 95/96 **Rugby League** ends with Wigan declared champions.

Stephen Hendry wins the **World Snooker Championship** and remains the world number one.

1997 At 21, Tiger Woods becomes the youngest **Masters** winner in history, as well as the first non-white winner at Augusta. He set the scoring record at 270 and the record for the largest margin of victory at 12 strokes.

1998 In Japan, **Curling** is included in the Winter Olympics for the first time.

1999 Pete Sampras beats his biggest rival, Andre Agassi in the **Wimbledon Men's Singles** Final giving him his sixth win at the All England Club.

In the **US Open Tennis** final, at the age of 17, Serena Williams beats the number one player Martina Hingis and marks the beginning of one of the most dominant careers in the history of women's tennis.

IN THE 1990s

THE DANGEROUS SIDE TO SPORT

By 1993, Monica Seles, the Serbian-American tennis player, had won eight Grand Slam titles and was ranked No. 1 in the world. On April 30, 1993, then just 19, she was sitting on a courtside seat during a changeover in a match in Hamburg when a German man, said later to be a fan of the tennis star's German rival, Steffi Graf, leaned over a fence and stabbed her between the shoulder blades with a knife. The assailant was quickly apprehended and Seles was taken to the hospital with a wound half and inch deep in her upper back. She recovered from her physical injuries but was left with deep emotional scars and didn't play again professionally for another two years.

Leading up to the 1994 Winter Olympics, figure skater Nancy Kerrigan was attacked during a practice session. This had been 'commissioned' by the ex-husband of fellow skater, Tonya Harding and her bodyguard. Kerrigan was Harding's long-time rival and the one person in the way of her making the Olympic team, and she was desperate to win. Fortunately for Kerrigan, the injury left her with just bruises – no broken bones but she had to withdraw from the U.S. Figure Skating Championship the following night. However, she was still given a spot on the Olympic team and finished with a silver medal. Harding finished in eighth place and later had her U.S. Figure Skating Championship title revoked and was banned from the United States Figure Skating Association for life.

Also in 1994, Andrés Escobar the Colombian footballer, nicknamed ' The Gentleman' - known for his clean style of play and calmness on the pitch - was murdered following a second-round match against the US in the FIFA World Cup. This was reportedly in retaliation for Escobar having scored an own goal which contributed to the team's elimination from the tournament.

In 1997, Evander Holyfield and Mike Tyson's fight made headlines after Tyson was disqualified for biting off a part of his rival's ear, an infamous incident that would lead to the event being dubbed "The Bite Fight".

The Sound and The Fury

Holyfield

VS.

Tyson II

WBA HEAVYWEIGHT CHAMPIONSHIP
Saturday, June 28
MGM GRAND GARDEN ARENA

www.holyfieldtyson.com

TRANSPORT

HAULAGE

The 1990s was a decade devoted to environmental considerations for haulage with top priority given to cleaner emissions and low noise levels. By the end of the decade, integrated IT solutions were being used to provide the tools necessary to increase efficiency and safety.

A significant factor in the 1990s was making the lorry more aerodynamic. A 20% saving in fuel consumption meant lower emissions and also the average transport operator could improve profits by up to 50%.

CRUISE SHIPS

The largest passenger ship of the 1990s was Royal Caribbean's 'Voyager of the Seas' at 137,276 gross tonnage and 310 m (1,020 ft) long.

This record was held between Oct 1999 and Sep 2000, when it was superseded by 'Explorer of the Seas', larger by only 12 GT. Royal Caribbean have, on order, and due 2024, an Oasis class cruiser of 231,000 gross tonnage, 362 m(1,188 ft) long.

THE HIGHWAY CODE

In July 1996 a separate written theory test was introduced to the Driving Test in the UK to replace questions asked about 'The Highway Code' whilst actually driving. Learner drivers were expected to know rather different information then from that published in the first edition of the Highway Code, price 1d, launched in 1931.

- In 1931 mirrors were not even mentioned.
- Drivers were advised to sound their horn when overtaking.
- At least 8 pages showed the various hand signals a driver should use. There was a single page in the current edition.
- Contained 18 pages (out of 24) of advice, compared to 135 pages in 2007.
- Included advice to drivers of horse drawn vehicles to 'rotate the whip above the head; then incline the whip to the right or left to show the direction in which the turn is to be made'.

It wasn't until the second edition of the Code that diagrams of road signs appeared, just 10 in all, plus a warning about the dangers of driving when tired or drinking and driving.

Renault Clio

Advertising for the first-generation Renault Clio introduced us to 'Nicole *et* Papa' and gave the small car a personality that appealed to drivers of all ages.

Ford Focus

The Focus replaced the previously very successful Escort. Ford wanted a 'World Car' to sell across all markets so the Focus was born and is still produced.

Toyota Previa

Toyota created the multi- purpose vehicle market with the Spacecruiser in the 80s, but the futuristic replacement, the Toyota Previa was a whole new approach to the people carrier.

Lexus LS 400

Toyota moved into the luxury market with the Lexus brand. The Lexus' flagship model is one of the most reliable vehicles ever built.

COCOTAXI

The auto-rickshaw began in Havana in the 1990s and soon spread to the whole of Cuba. These gas-scooters are named after their shape, that of a coconut and are made of a fibreglass shell with seats welded onto it. They can travel at about 30mph and because they are small, they weave and squeeze in and out of the city traffic. Blue Cocotaxis are for locals, yellow for tourists.

MOTORCYCLES

During the 1990s motorcycles started to evolve more quickly and there was a resurgence in the British biking industry with Triumph starting up production.

A bike lovers favourite however, was the 1995, Aprilia RS250.

NEW YEAR'S EVE 1999
The Millennium Bug

Whilst the world was getting 'ready to party' there was an undercurrent of anxiety about the Y2K (year 2000) Bug and many people were scared. When complicated computer programmes were first written in the 1960s, programmers used a two-digit code for the year, leaving out the "19." As the year 2000 approached, many believed that the systems would not interpret the "00" correctly, making the year 2000 indistinguishable from 1900 causing a major malfunction.

It was particularly worrying to certain organisations. Banks calculate the rate for interest owed daily and instead of the rate for one day, if the 'clocks went back' their computers would calculate a rate of interest for **minus** 100 years!

Airlines felt they were at a very great risk. All scheduled flights are recorded on computers and liable to be affected and, if the computer reverted to 1900, well, there were very few airline flights that year!
Power plants were threatened, depending on routine computer maintenance for safety checks, such as water pressure or radiation levels, the wrong date would wreck the calculations and possibly put nearby residents at risk.

Huge sums were spent to prepare for the consequences and both software and hardware companies raced to fix it by developing "Y2K compliant" programmes. Midnight passed on the 1 January 2000 and the crisis failed to materialise - planes did not fall from the sky, power stations did not melt down and thousands of people who had stocked up on food, water, even arms, or purchased backup generators or withdrawn large sums of money in anticipation of a computer-induced apocalypse, could breathe easily again.

The Millennium Dome

Officially called the O2, the huge construction and tourist attraction alongside the Thames in Greenwich, London was initially built to house an exhibition for the approach of the 21st Century. Designed by Sir Richard Rogers, the central dome is the largest in the world. On December 31, 1999, a New Year's Eve celebration at the dome was attended by some 10,500 people, including the Prime Minister, Tony Blair, and the Queen. Opening the next day, the Millennium Dome exhibition lasted until December 31, 2000.

AND A NEW MILLENNIUM

Memorabilia and Monuments

The Millennium Wheel Better known as the London Eye, at 135m (443 ft) it is Europe's tallest cantilevered observation wheel. Situated on the South Bank of the Thames when opened it used to offer the highest public viewing point in London until superseded in 2013 by the 245m high (804 ft) observation deck on the 72nd floor of The Shard.

Portsmouth's Millennium Tower opened five years late and officials were so concerned that people may actually have forgotten what the millennium was, that they gave it a new name, **The Spinnaker Tower**.

The Millennium Bridge is a steel suspension bridge for pedestrians over the River Thames linking Bankside with the City of London. Londoners nicknamed it the "Wobbly Bridge" after pedestrians experienced an alarming swaying motion on its opening day.

Lots of memorabilia was produced to mark the new millennium. Some pieces are timeless classics and others will soon be forgotten.

KEY EVENTS 2000-2009

2000:

Jan: Celebrations take place throughout the UK on the 1st and the Millennium Dome is officially opened by The Queen.

Aug 4th: Queen Elizabeth the Queen Mother celebrates her hundredth birthday

2001:

Feb: The Foot and Mouth disease crisis begins. Over 6 million cows and sheep are killed to halt the disease.

Jun: Labour wins the General Election. David Cameron is a new entrant, Edward Heath retires, and William Hague resigns as leader of the Conservatives.

2002:

Jan: The Euro is officially introduced in the Eurozone countries.

Jun: The Golden Jubilee. A special service is held in St Paul's Cathedral to mark the Queen's 50 years on the throne. Celebrations take place all over the country.

2003:

Mar: The United States, along with coalition forces primarily from the United Kingdom, initiates war on Iraq

May: BBC Radio 4 airs a report stating that the government claimed in its dossier, that Iraq could deploy weapons of mass destruction within forty-five minutes knowing the claim to be dubious.

Jul: Dr David Kelly, the weapons expert who was the reporter's source, is found dead.

2004:

Jan: The Hutton Inquiry into the circumstances of the death of Dr Kelly is published. The UK media, in general, condemns the report as a whitewash.

Jul: A new Countryside Code is published in advance of the 'Right to Roam' coming into effect in September across England and Wales.

TERRORISM

2001: On the 11th September, Al-Qaeda terrorists hijack civilian airliners and fly two into the Twin Towers of the World Trade Centre in New York, which collapse. There are 3,000 fatalities including 67 British nationals.

SOCIAL MEDIA

2004: In February, Mark Zuckerberg launches 'The Facebook', later renamed 'Facebook' as an online social networking website for Harvard University Students. In 2006 it was opened up to anyone over the age of 13.

EXPLOSION

2005: On the morning of 11 December, the UK experienced its largest explosion since World War Two. A huge blast at the Buncefield fuel depot in Hemel Hempstead, was heard as far away as the Netherlands and caused the UK's biggest blaze in peacetime which shrouded much of south-east England in smoke.

HIGH SPEED TRAINS

2007: In November, the Queen officially opened 'High Speed 1' and 'St Pancras International' station. The Channel Tunnel first opened to Eurostar in 1994, with trains running from Waterloo, but the new 69-mile link meant the journey from London to Paris reduced to 2 hrs 15 minutes and to Brussels 1 hr 51 min.

2005:
Apr: Prince Charles marries Camilla Parker Bowles at a private ceremony at Windsor Guildhall.

Aug: Hurricane Katrina devastates much of the U.S. Gulf Coast from Louisiana to the Florida Panhandle killing an estimated 1,836 people

2006:
Jul: Twitter is launched, becoming one of the largest social media platforms in the world.

Nov: Alexander Litvinenko a British-naturalised Russian defector dies of polonium poisoning in London.

2007:
Jun: Tony Blair resigns as Prime Minister and Gordon Brown is elected unopposed.

Jul: England introduces a ban on smoking in enclosed public places in line with Scotland, Wales and N. Ireland.

2008:
Mar: Terminal 5 is opened at London Heathrow but IT problems cause over 500 flights to be cancelled

Nov: St Hilda's College admits male undergraduates and ceases to be the last single-sex college at Oxford.

Dec: Woolworths shuts down in the UK.

2009:
Jul: The largest haul of Anglo-Saxon treasure ever found, the Staffordshire Hoard, is first uncovered buried beneath a field near Litchfield. 4,600 items amounting to 11 lb of gold, 3lb of silver and 3.5k pieces of garnet cloisonné jewellery.

Oct: The independent audit of MPs expenses is completed and exposes a widespread parliamentary scandal.

2010:

Jan: In the Chilcott Inquiry, set up in 2009, Tony Blair is questioned in public for the first time about his decision to take the UK to war against Iraq.

May: The General Election results in a Hung Parliament. An alliance is formed between the Tories and the Liberal Democrats.

2011:

Feb: An earthquake of 6.3 magnitude devastates Christchurch, New Zealand. Hundreds of people are killed.

Apr: Prince William marries Catherine Middleton in Westminster Abbey.

2012:

Jun: The UK begins celebrations of the Queen's Diamond Jubilee. Events include a pageant on the Thames and a Pop Concert outside Buckingham Palace

Jul: The summer Olympic Games are held in London, making it the first city to host them for a third time.

2013:

Jul: A new Marriage Act receives Royal Assent and same-sex marriage becomes legal in England and Wales.

Aug: A burger, grown from bovine stem cells in a laboratory, is cooked and eaten in London. The same month, a 15 ton 'fatburg' is removed after completely blocking a London sewer.

2014:

Mar: Prince Harry launches the Invictus Games for wounded soldiers.

Mar: The first gay weddings take place in England and Wales.

THE SHARD

2012: In July, The Shard, an iconic 'vertical city' is officially opened in London. It is the tallest building in Europe and the tallest habitable free-standing structure in the UK at 1,016ft (309.6 m)

THE ARAB SPRING

2010: 'The Arab Spring', a series of anti-government protests, uprisings, and armed rebellions spread across much of the Arab world. Starting in Tunisia it spread to Libya, Egypt, Yemen, Syria and Bahrain. Amongst leaders to be deposed was Gaddafi of Libya.

BREXIT

June 2016: After months of heated, angry argument and debate, the referendum on whether to leave the EU or remain within it, is held. Nearly 30m people take part and the result is to leave the EU: 51.9% votes to 48.1%.

March 2017: Article 50 is invoked and the two-year countdown to departure begins.

March 2019: Parliament rejected Theresa May's EU withdrawal agreement and a new deadline is set by The European Council to leave, with or without an Agreement, at the end of Oct 2019.

Jun 2019: Unable to 'deliver Brexit', Theresa May steps down and in Jul 2019: Boris Johnson becomes Prime Minister.

Oct 2019: The deadline to leave passes, and the EU agrees to a new date, end of Jan 2020. Commemorative Brexit coins are melted down.

Jan 2020: Johnson signs the Withdrawal Agreement.

January 31ˢᵗ 2020: At 11pm, the UK leaves the European Union and marks the moment with a party in Parliament Square.

2015:
Jan: Two Al-Qaeda gunmen kill 12 and injure 11 more at the Paris headquarters of the satirical newspaper Charlie Hebdo.

May: The General Election is won by David Cameron for the Conservatives with an outright majority of 331 seats.
Jun: The 800th anniversary of the Magna Carta.

2016:
Jun: The UK Referendum to leave the EU, Brexit, takes place and the majority vote is 'Yes'. David Cameron later resigns.
Jul: On July 14, Bastille Day (Independence Day), a terrorist drives a truck through a crowded promenade in Nice, France. 87 people are killed.
Nov: Donald Trump becomes US President.

2017:
There are a string of deadly terror attacks in Britain including : Westminster Bridge, the Manchester Arena and London Bridge.
Jun: The Tories lose their majority in Theresa May's general election gamble.

2018:
Apr: The UK, France, and United States order the bombing of Syrian military bases.

May: Prince Harry marries the American actress Meghan Markle in St George's Chapel, Windsor Castle. It is thought 1.9m people watched on TV worldwide.

2019:
Jun: Theresa May resigns as Prime Minister. Before she goes, she agrees a new legally binding target to reach net zero by 2050.
Jul: Boris Johnson becomes Prime Minister.

FILMS & THE ARTS

"One Ring to Rule Them All'

Based on the fantasy, adventure epics written by JRR Tolkein in the 1930s and 40s, Peter Jackson's trilogy of films became a major financial success, received widespread acclaim and is ranked among the greatest film trilogies ever made. The three films were shot simultaneously in Jackson's native New Zealand between 1999 and 2000 and with a budget of $281m, was one of the most ambitious film projects ever undertaken.

The **Lord of the Rings: The Fellowship of the Ring** was nominated for 13 Oscars and won four, one of which, unsurprisingly, was for the Special Effects as did **The Lord of the Rings: The Two Towers** and **The Lord of the Rings: The Return of the King**.

Peter Jackson then went on to make a further three films based on Tolkein's Middle Earth saga, **'The Hobbit: An Unexpected Journey, The Hobbit: The Desolation of Smaug** and **The Hobbit: The Battle of the Five Armies**. The three films were prequels to the Lord of the Rings saga and together, the six films became one of the 'greatest movie series franchise' of all time.

'The Greatest Fairy Tale Never Told'

In 2002, the Oscar for Best Animated Feature was awarded for the first time to **Shrek**, the large, surly, sarcastic, wisecracking, Scottish-accented greenish ogre with a round

face and stinky breath who took a mud shower outdoors near his home in the swamp and blew fart bubbles in a mud pool! But being a goodhearted ogre, children and adults alike, loved him!

'A Film of Our Times'

The Social Network made in 2010, is an American biographical drama portraying the founding of the social networking phenomenon Facebook and the resulting lawsuits. Based on the book, 'The Accidental Billionnaires' by

Ben Mezrich the film was nominated for the Oscars in 2011 winning The Best Adapted Screenplay but missing out on Best Picture to **The King's Speech**.

'Precious Pieces'

In 2007 Damien Hirst wowed the art-world with his fabulous **For the Love of God** a life-size platinum cast of an eighteenth century human skull, covered by 8,601 flawless diamonds, inset with the original skull's teeth. At the front of the cranium is a 52.4 carat pink

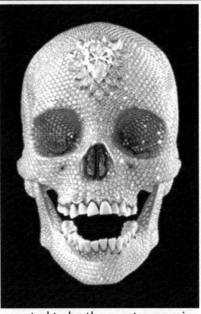

diamond. The work is reputed to be the most expensive contemporary artwork ever made and was *allegedly* entitled **For the Love of God** in response to a question posed by the artist's mother "For the love of God, what are you going to do next?"! It has become one of the most widely recognised works of contemporary art and represents the artist's continued interest in mortality and the fragility of life.

Screaming Success

In May, 2012, a pastel version of **The Scream**, by Norwegian painter Edvard Munch, sells for $120m in New York City, setting a new world record for a work of art at auction.

'Question Everything, Believe Nothing'

Conspiracy theory is not a new phenomenon but in 2001, Dan Brown introduced the world to Robert Langdon and a whole new collection of conspiracies and secret societies, with his first book, **Angels & Demons**. Set in the Vatican and Rome, Langdon must decipher a labyrinthine trail of ancient symbols if he is to defeat the Illuminati, a monstrous secret brotherhood.

When **The Da Vinci Code** came along in 2003, hordes of tourists descended on Paris, staring at the Mona Lisa as though she held the secret to life and traipsing around cathedrals and monuments, speculating on the Holy Grail and obsessed with the Priory of Sion and Opus Dei.

By 2009 in **The Lost Symbol**, Brown had set his sights on the Capitol Building, Washington DC and the shadowy, mythical world in which the Masonic secrets abound.

Back in Italy in 2013, this time Florence, for **Inferno**, Langdon is also back to hidden passageways and ancient secrets that lie behind historic facades, deciphering a sequence of codes buried deep within Renaissance artworks with only the help of a few lines from Dante's Inferno.

DAN BROWN

The phenomenal international bestseller

The Da Vinci CODE

'Blockbuster perfection'
NEW YORK TIMES

The Top Ten UK Singles of the 21st Century

YEAR

2013	**Happy** by Pharrell Williams.
2002	Will Young's **Anything is Possible**
2013	**Blurred Lines** sung by Robin Thicke featuring TI and Pharrell Williams.
2014	Mark Ronson and featuring Bruno Mars with **Uptown Funk**
2011	Adele singing **Someone Like You**
2011	**Moves Like Jagger** by Maroon 5 featuring Christina Aguilera
2012	Gotye featuring Kimbra and **Somebody That I Used to Know**
2013	**Wake Me Up** by Avicii
2009	The Black Eyed Peas with **I Gotta Feeling**
2013	Daft Punk featuring Pharrell Williams and **Get Lucky**

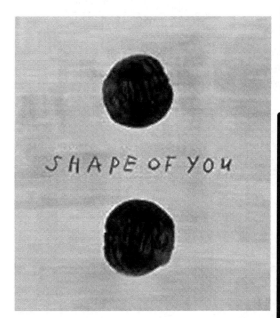

Since 2014 streaming has counted towards sales, called "combined sales", at the rate of 100 streams equal to one download or physical purchase, although the singles chart no longer uses this ratio. The biggest selling song of the 21st Century, based on combined physical, download and streaming sales, *and as of Sep 2017*, is **The Shape of You** by Ed Sheeran, (2017) with sales of just over 3 million.

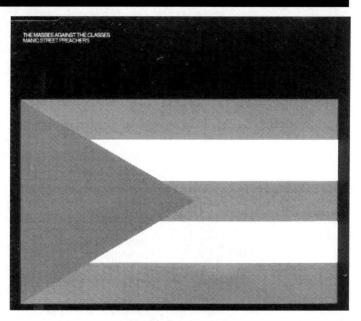

First of the Century

The first No 1 Single of the 21st Century in the UK Charts is **Manic Street Preachers** with The Masses Against the Classes. This song by Welsh rock band was released as a limited-edition single being deleted, removed from wholesale supply, on the day of release. Despite this, it peaked at No 1.

Millennial Music

What about the music the Millennials, born in the 80s and 90s, like to listen to? It may eventually fit just as well onto a "best songs of all time" playlist alongside the likes of The Beatles and The Supremes. These are some of the 21st-century pop songs that could stand the test of time and they are all female artists too!

Single Ladies (Put a Ring on It) by Beyoncé. **Umbrella** by Rihanna featuring Jay-Z. **Shake it Off** by Taylor Swift. **Toxic** by Britney Spears. **Rolling in the Deep** by Adele and **Firework** by Katy Perry.

However, those of us **Born in 1962** are not surprised to know, that in 2019, a US study found that golden oldies stick in millennials' minds far more than the relatively bland, homogeneous pop of today. A golden age of popular music lasted from the 1960s to the 1990s, academics claimed. Songs from this era proved to be much more memorable than tunes released in the 21st century.

FASHION

Music and fashion have been intertwined since the 1960s and nothing appears to be changing at the beginning of the 21st Century. The young will imitate their idols. Today though, designers are taking their inspiration from the past and bringing it back into the future, the new millennium fashion is a 'fusion' of the 60's, 70's and 80's, feeding our freedom to 'wear what we want, whenever we want'.

However, one major shift of emphasis will be the consumer's demand for environmental sustainability and social responsibility and to move away from 'fast, disposable fashion'. Fashion began moving at breakneck speeds in the 1960's, and the young wanted cheaply made clothing to follow these new trends. Fashion brands had to find ways to keep up with the ever-increasing demand for affordable clothing and this led to the massive growth in manufacturing being outsourced to the developing world, saving us millions of pounds in labour costs.

In the 21st Century we are aware of dreadful labour practices and the enormous amounts of waste. The industry will need to slow down for the customer mindful of how their clothes are made.

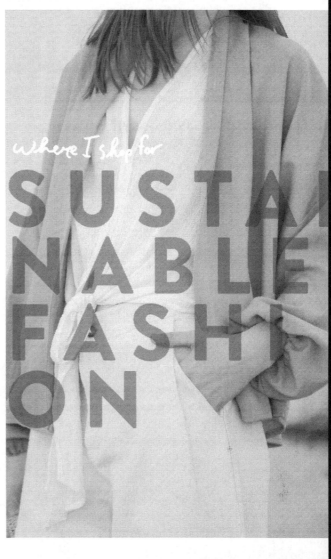

SCIENCE & TECHNOLOGY

Watch everywhere.

Stream unlimited movies and TV shows on your phone, tablet, laptop, and TV without paying more.

The technological innovations of the first two decades of the 21st century have drastically revolutionised people's day-to-day lives. Television, radio, paperback novels, cinemas, landline telephones and even letter writing can be, and have been by millions, replaced by connected devices, digital books, Netflix, and communications using apps such as Twitter, Facebook or Snapchat. We have marvels such as personalized hover boards, self-driving cars and, of course, the smartphone. All commonplace now when just a decade and a half ago most were unfathomable.

Consumers watch films, listen to music, record the day, book holidays and carry out their shopping with a few taps on a screen and even people who have never owned a computer are digitally connected 24-hours a day via their smartphones.

E-readers and Kindle

E-readers have been under development since the 1940s, but it was not until 2004 when Sony first brought out an e-reader, and then, when demand for e-books increased, Kindle arrived in 2007, that they became mainstream. An eBook is a text-based publication in digital form stored as electronic files. E-readers are small, convenient, light and have a huge storage capacity that allows for reading whilst

travelling, making electronic notes and character summaries and more. Pages do not exist in eBooks and where the reader is 'up to' is altered depending on what font size and layout the reader has chosen, which means 'your place' is displayed as a percentage of the whole text.

Although it was feared e-readers were the death knell for the traditional book, it appears not to be the case as it seems many people really do like to hold a physical book in their hands, feeling the weight. After all, even Kindle uses a **'bookmark'** to hold our place!

3D Printing

The 3D printer has been around since the 1980s. Now, the know-how is getting used for everything from automobile components to bridges to much less painful ballet slippers, synthetic organs, custom dental work, prosthetic limbs, and custom hearing aids.

The Future of Transport

Driverless Cars
Self-driving cars are expected to be on the roads more quickly, and in greater numbers, than was anticipated.

Floating Trains
There are already Maglev – magnetic levitation – trains in use. The Shanghai Maglev connects their Airport with a station on the outskirts of the city. At speeds up to 268 mph.

Hyperloop
High speed bullet trains or transport capsules are being developed to provide unprecedented speeds of 600mph.

Solar Panel Roads
Which also generate electricity are being tested in, amongst other countries, France, the US and China as well as on bike lanes in the Netherlands.

Touch Screens

Smartphones, tablets, and even Smartwatches all need one underlying technology without which they cannot succeed. The touch screen, as we know it integrated into consumer products, took off in the 2000s and is now everywhere, homes, cars, restaurants, shops, planes, wherever. Unlike other computer devices, touchscreens are unique because they allow the user to interact directly with what's on the screen, unlike a mouse that moves a cursor.

In 2007, the original iPhone was released and revolutionised the phone industry, its touchscreen can change between a dialling pad, a keyboard, a video, a game, or a myriad of other apps. The Apple iPad was released in 2010 and with it, a wave of tablets from competitors. Not only are most of our phones equipped with touchscreens, but portable computers are too.

2000 Tiger Woods wins the **US Open** golf by 15 shots, a record for all majors.

Australia wins the **Rugby League World Cup** against New Zealand. Italy joins the Five Nations **Rugby Union** making it the Six Nations.

2001 Sir Donald Bradman dies. He retains the highest **Test Match** batting average of 99.94.

Venus Williams wins the **Ladies Singles Final at Wimbledon**.

2002 "Lewis–Tyson: Is On". Lennox won the fight by a knockout to retain the **WBC Heavyweight Boxing** Crown.
Arsenal matched Manchester United with their third Double, **FA Cup** and **League title**.

2003 Mike Wier becomes the first Canadian and the first *left-handed golfer* to win the **Masters**.
Serena Williams beats her sister Venus in the **Ladies Singles Final at Wimbledon**.

2004 In Athens, Kelly Holmes wins **Olympic Gold** for the 800 & 1500m. Britain also win Gold in the 4x100m relay. M i c h a e l Schumacher, in his Ferrari, wins a record 12 of the first 13 races of the season, and wins the **F1** World Drivers Championship.

2005 Ellen MacArthur attains the World Record for **Sailing** the fastest solo circumnavigation of the globe.
In **Cricket**, England win The Ashes.

2006 Justin Gatlin equals Powell's **100m world record** time of 9.77 seconds in Quatar.
In golf, Europe wins the **Ryder Cup** for the third straight time, defeating the USA 18½–9½.

2007 27 January – After nearly 50 years, the final edition of **'Grandstand'**, the BBC flagship sports programme is aired.
Australia completes a 5–0 whitewash over England in the **Ashes Series**, the first time since 1920–21 that one team has won all the Tests in the series.

2008 At the Beijing Olympics, Team GB dominate the **Cycling**, winning 14 medals, including 8 Gold.
Usain Bolt thundered to victory in the **100m Olympic final** at the Bird's Nest in a world record time. He also broke the world record in the 200m.

2009 Jenson Button and Brawn GP secure their first and only **F1 Drivers' Championship** and Constructors' Championship titles, respectively.
In an incident that shocked the entire sporting world, the **Sri Lankan cricket team** was attacked by terrorists while heading to the stadium to play a match.

2010 At his debut in the US, Amir Khan, the British boxer retains his **WBA Light Welterweight** title for the second time.

Alberto Contador of Spain, wins his 3rd **Tour de France** and 5th Grand Tour.

2011 Rory McIlroy fired a 69 in the final round of the **US Open**, breaking the record with a 268 and winning by eight strokes. He becomes the youngest US Open winner since Bobby Jones in 1923.

2012 At the **London Olympics** on 'Super Saturday', Jessica Ennis-Hill, Greg Rutherford and Mo Farah all win gold in an unforgettable 44 minutes inside the Olympic Stadium. On this one single day twelve British athletes win gold medals across six events

Bradley Wiggins wins the **Tour de France**, the first British rider ever to do so and Mark Cavendish wins the final stage on the Champs-Élysées for a record fourth successive year.

2013 The **Boston Marathon** is bombed by terrorists. At **Wimbldon**, Andy Murray defeats Novak Djokovic to become the first British winner of the **Men's Singles** since Fred Perry in 1936. He earns his second Grand Slam title

2014 The first ever Invictus Games is hosted in London with over 400 competitors from 13 nations. The FA Cup Final is won by Arsenal, a joint record 11th Cup having beaten Hull City 4-3 after extra time.

2015 In Golf, Jordan Spieth led from the start in the **Masters**, shooting a record-tying 270, 18 under, to win his first major at the age of 21. Later in the year he also wins the U.S. Open.

The **Grand National** at Aintree is won by 'Many Clouds' ridden by Leighton Aspell, his second consecutive Grand National Victory.

2016 Leicester City, 5,000-1 outsiders for the title, win the **Premier League.**

Former Leicester City player Gary Lineker stated that if Leicester won the league, he would present Match of the Day in his underwear!

2017 Roger Federer becomes the undisputed **King of Wimbledon** with his record 8th win.

Chris Froome wins his 4th **Tour de France**.

In the **Women's World Cup Cricket**, England beat India by nine runs in the final at Lords.

2018 The **Tour de France** general classification was won by Geraint Thomas of Team Sky, his first win.

Roger Bannister, the first man to run a four-minute mile died this year.

2019 At the **Cheltenham Festival**, 'Frodon' ridden by Bryony Frost wins the Ryanair Chase. She is the first woman to ride a Grade One winner at Cheltenham.

Tiger Woods wins his first major in 11 years at the **Masters**.

2020 At the Tokyo Olympics, Lamont Jacobs wins the **100m** sprint and is the new '**World's Fastest Man**'.

1947: Britain was struck this year by 'the perfect storm'. Record snowfall followed by a sudden thaw which culminated in heavy rain produced what is widely considered to be Britain's worst flood. Over 100,000 homes were directly affected and over 750,000 hectares of farmland submerged. The damages at the time totalled around £12 million, £300 million in today's terms.

1952: In August, the tiny village of Lynmouth, north Devon, suffered the worst river flood in English history. On the 15th, just over 9in (230mm) of rain fell over north Devon and west Somerset. The East and West Lyn rivers flooded and tons of water, soil, boulders and vegetation descended over Exmoor to meet at sea level in Lynmouth. The village was destroyed. The West Lyn rose 60 ft (18.25 m) above the normal level at its highest point and 34 people lost their lives.

1953: The great North Sea flood of January caused catastrophic damage and loss of life in Scotland, England, Belgium and The Netherlands and was Britain's worst peacetime disaster on record claiming the lives of 307 people. There were no severe flood warnings in place and the combination of gale-force winds, low pressure and high tides brought havoc to over 1,000 miles of coastline and 32,000 people were displaced because of flooding.

1963: Britain had the coldest winter in living memory, lasting for three long months from Dec 1962. The 6th March 1963 was the first morning of the year without frost anywhere in Britain.
It was so cold that rivers, lakes and even the sea froze over. On 25 February a record low of -22c in Braemar was recorded and 95,000 miles of road were snowbound.

1987: The Hurricane that wasn't supposed to be! Weatherman Michael Fish, like other forecasters, didn't see it coming. Eighteen people died and over 15 million trees were lost when in October, the hurricane-force winds blasted through south-east England. Meteorological research revealed a completely new weather phenomenon called the 'sting jet', a 100mph wind, the first to be documented in Britain.

WEATHER

2003: In August a new UK record was set for the 'Hottest Day in History' when temperatures reached 38.5c (101.3f) in Faversham, Kent. By the end of the summer, the heat had claimed the lives of over 2,000 people in Britain, mostly through heat stroke or dehydration.

An almost empty reservoir

1976: Britain had its hottest three months in living memory and it should have been the perfect summer, but with the continued sunshine came the worst drought in 150 years. Rivers dried up, soil began to crack and water supplies were on the verge of running out in Britain's most dramatic heatwave of the 20th Century. The drought was so rare, Britain appointed its first ever minister for drought, Denis Howell. He was nicknamed the minister for rain as the day after they installed him the heavens opened for the next two months!

2000: Following a wet spring and early summer, the autumn was the wettest on record for over 270 years. Repeated heavy rainfall in October and November caused significant and extensive flooding, inundated 10,000 homes and businesses. Train services cancelled, major motorways closed, and power supplies disrupted.

2007: Summer 2007 was the wettest on record with 414.1mm of rain falling across England and Wales in May, June and July - more than at any time since records began in 1766.
Although the rain was exceptionally heavy, climatologists say it was not the result of global warming. A report by the Centre for Ecology and Hydrology concluded the rain was a freak event, not part of any historical trend.

2004: A flash flood submerged the Cornish village of Boscastle during the busy holiday period when over 60 mm of rain (typically a month's rainfall) fell in two hours. The ground was already saturated due to two weeks of above average rainfall and the Jordan and Valency rivers burst their banks causing about two billion litres of water to rush down the valley straight into Boscastle. This led to the flash flood which caused total devastation to the area, but miraculously, no loss of life.

GLOBAL DISASTERS OF

Australian Bush Fires

Australia experienced the worst bushfire season ever in 2019-2020 with fires blazing for months in large parts of the country. Around 126,000 square kilometres of land and thousands of buildings were destroyed and at least 33 people died. Victoria and New South Wales were the worst affected and a state of emergency was declared in the capital city, Canberra.

Australia is used to bushfires, they are a natural part of the country's summer and native trees like eucalyptus need the heat for their seeds to be released, but this season they started earlier than usual, spread much faster, burned hotter and lasted longer, from June 2019 until March 2020, with the worst of the fires happening in December and January.

2019 was Australia's hottest and driest year on record with temperatures hitting 40c and above in every state and these hot, dry and windy conditions made the fires bigger and more intense than normal.

THE INDIAN OCEAN TSUNAMI

In the early morning of December 26, 2004, there was a massive and sudden movement of the Earth's crust under the Indian Ocean. This earthquake was recorded at magnitude 9 on the Richter Scale and as it happened under the ocean, the sea floor was pushed upwards, by as much as 40m, displacing a huge volume of water and causing the devastating tsunami which hit the shores of Indonesia, Sri Lanka, India, Thailand, and the Maldives.

Within 20 minutes the waves, reaching 30 feet high, and racing at the speed of a jet aircraft, engulfed the shoreline of Banda Aceh on the northern tip of Sumatra, killing more than 100,000 people and pounding the city into rubble. Then, moving on to Thailand, India and Sri Lanka, an estimated total of 250,000 people were killed, including many tourists on the beaches of Thailand. Millions more people were displaced, and eight hours later, and 5,000 miles from its Asian epicentre, the tsunami claimed its final casualties on the coast of South Africa.

THE 21ST CENTURY

Hurricane Katrina

Hurricane Katrina hit the coast of Louisiana on 29th August 2005. A Category 3 storm, it caused destruction from central Florida to Texas, but most lives were lost, and damage caused in New Orleans. It passed over Miami where the 80mph winds uprooted trees and killed two people. Hurricanes need warm ocean water to keep up speed and strength, so Katrina weakened whilst over the land to a tropical storm. Crossing back into the Gulf of Mexico, it quickly regained hurricane status and at its largest, was so wide, its diameter stretched

right across the Gulf. Katrina crossed back over the coast near Biloxi, Mississippi, where winds were the strongest and damage was extensive. However, later that morning, the first of 50 old levees broke in New Orleans, and a surge of floodwater poured into the low-lying city.

COVID 19 A GLOBAL PANDEMIC

The first human cases of COVID-19, the coronavirus disease caused by SARS CoV-2, were first reported from Wuhan City, China, in December 2019. Environmental samples taken in a food market in Wuhan where wild and farmed animals were traded, were positive for the virus and it is still unconfirmed whether the market was the origin of the virus or was just the setting for its initial spread.

The virus spread rapidly throughout China and has been found in 202 other countries, reaching Britain, from Europe, in late January 2020 and in March, the 'Stay at Home Order' or lockdown, was introduced. Non-essential travel was banned, schools were shut along with many businesses and venues. We were told to stay 6ft apart from others, self-isolate and, if at risk, to shield.

1953 Calendar

January

S	M	T	W	T	F	S
				1	2	3
4	5	6	7	8	9	10
11	12	13	14	15	16	17
18	19	20	21	22	23	24
25	26	27	28	29	30	31

February

S	M	T	W	T	F	S
1	2	3	4	5	6	7
8	9	10	11	12	13	14
15	16	17	18	19	20	21
22	23	24	25	26	27	28

March

S	M	T	W	T	F	S
1	2	3	4	5	6	7
8	9	10	11	12	13	14
15	16	17	18	19	20	21
22	23	24	25	26	27	28
29	30	31				

April

S	M	T	W	T	F	S
			1	2	3	4
5	6	7	8	9	10	11
12	13	14	15	16	17	18
19	20	21	22	23	24	25
26	27	28	29	30		

May

S	M	T	W	T	F	S
					1	2
3	4	5	6	7	8	9
10	11	12	13	14	15	16
17	18	19	20	21	22	23
24	25	26	27	28	29	30
31						

June

S	M	T	W	T	F	S
	1	2	3	4	5	6
7	8	9	10	11	12	13
14	15	16	17	18	19	20
21	22	23	24	25	26	27
28	29	30				

July

S	M	T	W	T	F	S
			1	2	3	4
5	6	7	8	9	10	11
12	13	14	15	16	17	18
19	20	21	22	23	24	25
26	27	28	29	30	31	

August

S	M	T	W	T	F	S
						1
2	3	4	5	6	7	8
9	10	11	12	13	14	15
16	17	18	19	20	21	22
23	24	25	26	27	28	29
30	31					

September

S	M	T	W	T	F	S
		1	2	3	4	5
6	7	8	9	10	11	12
13	14	15	16	17	18	19
20	21	22	23	24	25	26
27	28	29	30			

October

S	M	T	W	T	F	S
				1	2	3
4	5	6	7	8	9	10
11	12	13	14	15	16	17
18	19	20	21	22	23	24
25	26	27	28	29	30	31

November

S	M	T	W	T	F	S
1	2	3	4	5	6	7
8	9	10	11	12	13	14
15	16	17	18	19	20	21
22	23	24	25	26	27	28
29	30					

December

S	M	T	W	T	F	S
		1	2	3	4	5
6	7	8	9	10	11	12
13	14	15	16	17	18	19
20	21	22	23	24	25	26
27	28	29	30	31		

Printed in Poland
by Amazon Fulfillment
Poland Sp. z o.o., Wrocław
29 December 2022

18d5ada7-1e50-4c21-9a38-c4db4f3ab0abR01